Prai...

"Any business writer who ...... help .... a .... emphatically should rea... .... practical, stylishly writte... .... else."

C. Michael Curtis
Senior Editor
The Atlantic Monthly

"At Liberty Mutual, we consider what we write to be part of our brand image. The principles in *Words at Work* have helped us to communicate more clearly and persuasively to our customers as well as to ourselves. Frankly, it's refreshing to discover that people can actually enjoy reading what an insurance company writes! And Susan Benjamin is the Vince Lombardi of writing coaches—tough, fair, and oh so effective."

Stephen G. Sullivan
Senior Vice President
Liberty Mutual Insurance Company

"As a communications director and attorney, I recommend the *Words at Work* process to anyone writing to make a point. I've seen entire teams of writers, with wide ranges of skill, transform their work using this approach.

"In today's corporate environment, you need to constantly demonstrate how you add value. This writing process frees you to focus on understanding the business messages you need to communicate. You spend less time writing, so you can exercise greater influence as a strategist."

Michele Jalbert
Director, Communications
Polaroid Corporation

Words at Work

*Business Writing in Half the Time
with Twice the Power*

Susan Benjamin
founder, Words at Work

Addison-Wesley
Reading, Massachusetts

Many of the designations used by manufacturers and sellers to distinguish their products are claimed as trademarks. Where those designations appear in this book and Addison-Wesley was aware of a trademark claim, the designations have been printed in initial capital letters (e.g., Xerox).

Library of Congress Cataloging-in-Publication Data

Benjamin, Susan, 1957–
    Words at work : business writing in half the time with twice the
    power / Susan Benjamin.
        p.   cm.
    Includes index.
    ISBN 0–201–15484–6 (alk. paper)
    1. Business writing.   I. Title
    HF5718.3.B46   1997
    808´.06665—dc21   97–18551
                                                                          CIP

Addison-Wesley is an imprint of Addison Wesley Longman, Inc.
Cover design by Suzanne Heiser
Text design by Dede Cummings
Set in 11-point Minion by A&B Typesetters

1 2 3 4 5 6 7 8 9-MA-0100999897
First printing, August 1997

Addison-Wesley books are available at special discounts for bulk purchases in the U.S. by corporations, institutions and other organizations. For more information, please contact the Corporate, Government, and Special Sales Department at Addison Wesley Longman, Inc., One Jacob Way, Reading, MA 01867, or call (800) 238–9682.

Find us on the World Wide Web at http://www.aw.com/gb/

*To my many clients and students who taught me so much
while learning to improve their writing*

Contents

Acknowledgments

As the old saying goes, "I couldn't have done it without them." In this case, "them" refers to quite a few enthusiastic and word-conscious people. First are my agent, Lisa Ross, who patiently, even willingly, listened to my ideas, and my editor, John Bell, whose invaluable advice about writing extends well beyond books.

In addition, I cannot express my indebtedness to all those enthusiastic players who understand the importance of high-quality writing at Liberty Mutual; John Hancock Group; the various Blue Cross and Blue Shield organizations; Polaroid; Mass Envelope, Plus; Summit Strategies; Pioneer Investments; VHB; Nichols Aircraft; and many others. In particular, thank you Ron Coyne, Steve Sullivan, John Cusolito, Ann Marie Doherty, Carl Mueller, Linda Newton, Ken Albert, Pat Ficociello, Michele Jalbert, Bob Rotchford, Steven Grossman, John Houghton, Jack Lyons, Joyce Gavenda, Tom Kucharvy, and, of course, Mary Sommer, for her professionalism and humor.

Special thanks to Mary Kleeman, client and dutiful friend; business guru Tom Peters, for spreading the word about Words at Work; and *The Atlantic Monthly* editor, Michael Curtis, for teaching me so much. Also much appreciation to those folks in the academic world of Berklee College of Music: Ron Bently, Charles Combs, Eric Kristensen, Reggie Loftin, and Lee Berk.

On the home front, thanks to Peter Quandt and Robert Capra for their interest and ideas; Pat Pattison, for his guidance and support for so many years; everyone at The Bookstore, in Gloucester, who answered my calls and endless questions. Marty Federman, great friend, expert writer, full-time office manager, and all-time great baby-sitter; and all those other Words at Work employees and contractors.

And finally, thanks all around to everyone who helped with the day-to-day and month-to-month activities so I could write this book and live a full and even—occasionally—relaxed life: my parents, for baby-sitting and house helping; Ilana Federman and Gemma Lymn for their patience and great baby care; Emerson Dahmen and Janet Grover for their love, friendship, rosemary pizzas, and so, so much else; and Adam Yosef Benjamin for his very presence, so full of everything good, in my life.

The Must-Read Introduction

WHY YOU MUST WRITE
BETTER DOCUMENTS FASTER!

Fast. That's how the business world approaches writing. Pondering a message before setting finger to keyboard—a relic from yesterday. Writing, rewriting, and rewriting again—a luxury reserved for English composition classes. And missed deadlines? Death to any organization, whether a 2-person business or a 25,000-employee corporation. Today you must get your messages out in record time, sometimes literally minutes after speaking with a client or attending a meeting.

But that's only half the problem. These quickly written documents must be livelier, more interesting, and more immediately intriguing to readers than ever before. In fact, if the average letter isn't captivating within the first *five* words, the readers either skim the message or throw it away. Why? Consider these facts:

- *The average reader watches four to eight hours of television daily.* Most of the images people spend so much time watching flash every two to three seconds—at the slowest. These images are provocative, too, darting from murdered bodies to couples in bed. Furthermore, most readers spend considerable TV time clicking the remote. I know a professor of literature and poetry who holds a Ph.D. in philosophy. On weekends, this connoisseur of contemporary language stations himself on the couch, clicker in hand, riding the on-air waves. Once, I timed the moments this otherwise patient man allowed between clicks. He gave each show approximately one second to catch his attention before he hurried on to a new channel. My friend's high-speed race across the television networks is typical of your readers' viewing habits. And you, with every business document you create, must somehow compete.

- *The typical American regularly reads quick communications, such as E-mail, speed memos, and* USA Today. When people do read longer works, they primarily favor high-drama novels that get a steel grip on their attention. The result is twofold: readers expect to get to the heart of the message, whether about stocks, foreign policy, or the weather, in moments; and they want the content to be interesting from the opening few words to the finale.

- *The average businessperson has significantly more documents to read than did the businessperson of 20 years ago—and significantly less time in which to read them.* Your readers are so inundated, they

---

Essential Benefits of *Words at Work*

How can you write faster without placing quality on the sacrificial block? The answer, as numerous businesspeople can testify, lies in the six steps in *Words at Work*: listing, writing, rewriting for structure, editing for word use, showing your work to get feedback, and proofreading. Following these steps conscientiously, you can

- *Cut your writing time significantly.* Businesspeople from major insurance organizations, consulting firms, and manufacturing companies as well as innumerable small businesses have slashed their writing time within weeks.

- *Create better documents.* Yes, it's true. As you write faster, the recipe in *Words at Work* will actually help you write *better* documents, from fact-filled proposals to snappy sales letters to compelling newsletter articles.

- *Permanently improve your writing style.* By using the "look, don't read" method of revision and other unique tips in this book, your writing style will dramatically improve *as* you write faster.

---

won't turn to the second page of a letter, read a brochure that doesn't immediately show a concrete advantage, or read a full set of instructions, regardless of their importance.

Few businesspeople know how to contend with the fast pace of today's business writing. During high school and college, we spent little if any time learning ways to quickly create the types of communications audiences demand. Some of those lessons may even have instilled poor writing habits. Rummage through your memory banks and pull out the outline, complete with numerals, numbers, and a,b,c's. Rather than go through the tiresome, not-to-mention time-consuming, process of creating an outline, most businesspeople simply sit down and write. The result: a piece as solid and dependable as a sand castle in high tide.

Of course, we can't just blame our teachers, curriculum developers, or textbook writers; they could hardly anticipate the lightning pulse of today's business community. Ten years ago, for example, who knew E-mail would rip through America, making instant responses to messages from New York to Normandy as common as instant oatmeal? But, as *Words at Work* proves, you can reeducate yourself each time you write while creating documents that get the right reader response.

HOW TO GAIN MAXIMUM BENEFIT FROM THIS BOOK

Writing does not follow a mix-and-serve recipe of scrambling words on the page to get a finished product. Rather, it's much like baking a pie; unless you go through every stage, from mixing the ingredients, to baking and letting it cool, you can't very well serve it. Compare pie baking to each of the six stages in this book:

1. Making a quick list of the most important points = laying out the ingredients.
2. Writing the document = mixing the ingredients.

3. Revising for structure = making the crust.
4. Revising for word use = baking the pie.
5. Showing for feedback and objectivity = letting the pie cool.
6. Checking for punctuation and small mistakes = cutting the pieces.

Most people in the business community don't complete the entire process. In fact, most don't go beyond the old write-once-and-I'm-finished routine or the okay-I-glanced-at-my-draft-I-must-have-rewritten-it approach. Essentially, in disseminating their documents, these people are serving a raw pie. And, just as you wouldn't expect dinner guests to eat uncooked dough and soupy filling, you shouldn't expect your readers to savor—or even to read—a half-baked document. Let *Words at Work* be your cookbook, taking you from the first stage of the writing process to the last.

Start by creating a portfolio of the documents you write every day, whether one-page letters, one-paragraph memos, or five-page articles. Set them aside in a file either on your computer or in your file cabinet. Then use *Words at Work* in these ways.

1. As an entire process

By taking each of the six steps in this book, you'll speed up your process while creating solid structure, lively word use, a professional and personal tone, and more. No need to read the whole book before beginning—you can immediately apply the strategies to your day-to-day writing as you go along. Have questions? Feel stumped? Check the troubleshooting section in each chapter for solutions.

2. As a troubleshooting device

Perhaps you've mastered most of the stages in this book. Maybe your coworkers model their letters and memos after yours and stop by your desk for advice when they have writing problems. Everything is fine, *except* you need twice as much time to write as everyone else does. And . . . well, perhaps you struggle with opening paragraphs. For solutions, focus on steps 1, 2, and 3 of this book. Then, as other writing problems flare up, as they inevitably will, smother them with the essential information you'll find there.

3. As a checklist for critical writing rights and wrongs

This book is loaded with checklists on everything from single words that replace strings of weaker ones to the top ten most tired letter openings and their lively alternatives. Stuck? Uncertain? Just open this book and get the information you need.

What Else?

In addition to the strategies in *Words at Work*, you can improve writing by

- *Taking classes.* Update and refine your skills, preferably in adult education programs at a local college. Be sure the professor provides intensive feedback and is willing to look at materials from your work.

- *Finding mentors.* Feedback is critical to changing writing habits. Be sure to get concrete and focused information from someone well connected to the writing world. In-house editors and technical writers can be great sources.

- *Reading.* Reading is a great way to learn what your reader wants. Start with magazines and newspapers. Look at the style, the variety of words, and sentence structure. Then, see if your writing is doing the same thing. Beware of comparing your writing to that of others in the business community. There's a lot of tired writing out there. Yours should be better—not equal.

- *Using common sense.* Ask yourself what your readers want. The answers are easy. Interesting word use; a personal, exciting message; information that applies directly to them. Then, see if your writing provides these things.

Listing

Object: *To virtually eliminate the difficulty of creating structure, one of the most complicated and time-consuming aspects of the writing process. Listing can also significantly shorten your actual writing time and help you create strong, coherent language.*

Structure: one of the biggest writing problems businesspeople confront. Whether reading a 1-page letter or a 50-page report, your readers must move from point to point as effortlessly as zooming along an empty freeway. Otherwise, they'll put the document away, opting for one of the dozens of other documents that clutter their desktops. Yet, revising structural problems can be a laborious and time-consuming task, taking up to an hour for a one-page letter and an afternoon or longer for a simple, five-page report.

The best way to create solid structure without expending extra editing time is through the fast and simple process of listing. The real beauty of listing, though, is that it ultimately saves you anywhere from five minutes to several hours.

Q&A: Revealing the Simple Sides of Listing

The following answers to my clients' most common questions reveal how a simple list can create multiple advantages.

What is listing?

Listing is simple—just write the main points that belong in your document. You can use whole sentences if you like, but you're better off using a few words or phrases. That way, you won't waste time formulating correct sentence structure. You'll also have an easier time adjusting the structure and can grasp each point at a glance.

How long should I spend writing my list?

Less time than you need to make a cup of coffee, look up a phone number and dial it, or search for a word in the dictionary. Listing a letter or short report should take seconds. Longer documents— minutes. Remember, don't think, strategize, or labor over details. Just get the ideas on the page as quickly as you would drop an ice cube into a glass of water. The results will be as clear, too!

How is listing different from the outlines I learned about in high school?

Outlines, as you probably recall, consist of as much wordplay as crossword puzzles, with none of the fun. These drawn-out plans were laden with Roman numerals announcing each point and endless letters and numbers beneath. Outlines also destroyed one of the elements most important to creating a lively, spirited voice: spontaneity. With listing, you jot down a few words, saving the real writing for later.

Do I use lists for each paragraph or for the entire document?

Obviously, you don't need to list the information in each paragraph of a 300-page manual. However, if you're writing a fax memo containing complex instructions, such as how to install an alarm or repair a broken heating system, in three paragraphs or less, you probably should write a list for each paragraph. Generally, follow these rules:

- *Letters and memos*: List the main points for the entire document.
- *Reports and proposals of 2–5 pages*: List the main points for the entire document.
- *Reports, proposals, and manuals of 5–25 pages*: List the main points for the entire document. Then, list the main points for each section.
- *Reports, proposals, and manuals over 25 pages*: List the main points for the entire document. Then, write a separate list for each chapter and, possibly, for each section of a chapter.

Should I ever include details in my list?

For most letters and shorter documents, you need only a few words per point when you list. No details. No elaboration. However, you may want to add a few details because you are

- uncertain about the information each point should contain
- afraid you have more details than you can manage
- afraid you'll forget certain points if you wait for even five or ten minutes before you write

In these cases, just add a few words beneath each item on your list. Remember, speed is everything, so don't bother with full sentences or even correct grammar and spelling.

Where do I write my list?

Write it anywhere—on a scrap piece of paper or the back of a data sheet. Some people keep their lists at the bottom of the computer screen, deleting each point as they write it in their document. This gives them a feeling of accomplishment as the list grows smaller and smaller. Others tape their lists over their desks or keep them in a separate file, notebook, or folder, referring to them as they go along. This approach is especially useful for longer documents that require more planning.

What if I don't want to follow my list once I start writing?

Remember, a list is a useful tool to glide you from point to point; it is not a marriage contract. Don't like your list? Create a new one. Or work with the one you have, adding points, removing points, regardless of how far you stray from the original ideas. In fact, you should probably revise your list as you progress to accommodate spontaneity.

What if I want to go off on a tangent once I'm writing?

Go ahead. After all, tangents are extremely valuable for your writing. They uncover thoughts and information you didn't know were there. They help the writing process flow. Just be sure to insert your major points into your list so you have a clear sense of your new direction and can cut and paste quickly and smoothly later.

Why is listing so helpful?

Take a look at these three reasons:

1. Once you write your list, your thoughts flow faster and the words tumble from one point to the next. You don't have to pause, wondering which point should come next, or check for potentially forgotten information.

2. Since you know where each point belongs, you won't inadvertently repeat yourself. Of the thousands of letters my company has edited for client corporations, 75 percent have anywhere from one line to several paragraphs of redundancies. Imagine how much wasted time that represents.

3. By placing your points in a reasonable order, you won't have to make major structural revisions later. This could mean the difference between minutes or even hours of work for lengthy reports and proposals.

Exit Lights—The Key to Structure

To get a real understanding of why listing is so important, consider this anecdote:

> When I was in the ninth grade, I played on the school soccer team. One day after practice I headed for the girls' locker room. I don't remember why, but the locker room was empty. As I entered, the door slammed behind me, sealing me in utter darkness. No exit sign lit in reassuring red. No distant lights leading to toilet or shower. Nothing but complete and impenetrable black. At that moment, I lost all sense of balance and direction, fumbling through the darkness, uncertain of whether I would bump into a locker, fall into an open doorway, bang against an open locker door. Eventually, my hand found the metallic bulb of the doorknob and I was liberated.

Writing is much like being locked in a dark room. You lose all sense of direction, unsure of whether you'll bump into the wrong points, fall into a tangent, or bang against old, irrelevant ideas as you fumble toward your message. By listing your main points before you write, you're creating spotlights illuminating the steps to a well-structured document.

ORDER AND REORDER: A QUICK TRIP TO A SUCCESSFUL LIST

Getting your thoughts down on paper is only one part of the listing stage. But don't worry! The next stage is equally easy: imposing some sort of order on your list.

One of the fastest ways to list is simply to drop your points on the page, numbering as you go. Say you work for a health insurance company. The one factor that distinguishes your company from the competition isn't cost (the government determines that), accessibility (your biggest competitor stares from the glassy windows across the street), or size (you're the biggest in the state), but customer service. In writing a letter about your customer service representatives you'd certainly mention these points:

1. Friendly manner on the telephone
2. Thorough knowledge of service
3. Calm disposition even during crises
4. Willingness to work overtime for the customer

The next step is *extremely* important. Ask yourself which points would interest your readers most. Then shift your list by simply crossing out old numbers and writing new ones beside them, making adjustments for each new audience. Remember, since your readers typically pay closest attention to information in the first few lines, make sure you intrigue them immediately. A dry, uninteresting opening point will surely be a one-way ticket to the wastebasket for your document.

Here's how you would reorder your customer service list:

3. 1. Friendly manner on the telephone
1. 2. Thorough knowledge of service
4. 3. Calm disposition even during crises
2. 4. Willingness to work overtime for the customer

Asks and Don't Asks When Reordering Your List

Ask Yourself

Which points most benefit my readers?

Which points address current concerns?

Which points distinguish my company from the competition?

Don't Ask Yourself

Which points interest me most?

Which points does the company usually accentuate?

Which points are easiest to write about?

Why Impose Order?

Because writing is an unnatural act. Think about your normal thought processes. You usually jump from point to point, thinking first of your department's budget, then about a difficult coworker, then about what you'll have for lunch, and back again to your department's budget. In conversation you probably do the same, talking about the movie you saw over the weekend, your vacation plans, then about a newsletter article you read two weeks earlier.

This ricochet process is normal enough. Unfortunately, when you write, your thoughts bounce around the page in a similar fashion. Yet your readers want a smooth, logical flow of information. After all, they can hardly rely on your gestures, the rise and fall of your voice, or their own participation in the discussion to carry them from point to point. Nor can they interrupt, ask questions, or ask you to repeat a point when you've shifted from one subject to another. That's why you must impose some sort of order, however unnatural, to your thoughts.

Now, take a look at why.

1. Thorough knowledge of service. Customers usually call because they don't understand a procedure, need more information about a process, or are upset about a product or service. Thanks to the knowledge your representatives have gleaned through first-rate training and years of experience, they can help customers—usually in a single phone call.

2. Willingness to work overtime for the customer. Your employees don't have a meager eight-hour commitment to the customer. Rather, they're on call from 7:00 A.M. to 10:00 P.M. every weekday and 9:00 A.M. to 5:00 P.M. on weekends. Keep this point second on the list, where, chances are, your readers will see it.

3. *Friendly manner on the telephone.* Friendliness is important. But a great attitude doesn't solve problems or get results. This important point belongs third on your list, where it is available for the reader, but not in a critical position on the page.

4. *Calm disposition even during crises.* Ah, this one is tricky. In admitting that your customer service representatives are calm during a crisis, you're admitting that crises exist. Of course, they *do* exist, in your company and everyone else's company. Without them, customer service departments would probably consist of one or two people playing solitaire in some small back room. But do you really want to call attention to these crises? My advice—get rid of this point altogether. But if you *must*, place it at the end of the list where your readers are less likely to see it.

Here's how your letter would look:

> Dear _____ ,
>
> You've been there. Calling another company for answers to your health care questions. You get put on hold, wait, and wait some more. Finally, a nameless representative says she'll call you back later. When? The next day. Or the day after that. Now—with HealthRight Insurance—wait no more.
>
> Our representatives have at least five years of experience in numerous health insurance areas and regularly attend classes on everything from industry changes to new regulations. That means you'll get your vital information fast—usually within a single phone call. And they're available more often than most other companies' representatives—from 7:00 A.M. to 11:00 P.M. every weekday and 9:00 to 5:00 on weekends. Need help other times? Just call our 24-hour hotline at 555-1212. Regardless of when you call, our representatives will be courteous and calm—so you can feel calm, too.

If you would like to know more, just call our office at
555-1213.

Sincerely,

Mary Ann Lonner
Manager, Customer Service Department

Now, look at a second way of ordering the list. The audience: still customers. Your reason for writing: to show your customer service representatives' level of professionalism. Your order: most important to least important information. The information: identical to that in the first letter. Only now, the scenario is different:

> The city newspaper nearly bubbled with excitement over a recent scandal when a customer took a health insurance company—not yours, fortunately—to court. She claimed her interactions with customer service representatives were so horrible that the stress exacerbated her illness and interfered with her work and family life. She cried emotional and physical damages. Little came of the suit except an investigation into the industry's customer service practices.

To reassure your customers, you send a letter, organizing the points in this way:

1. *Calm disposition even during crises.* Your customer service representatives calm heated situations faster than the New York City fire department. They ensure that every situation gets resolved quickly and easily, with minimal customer involvement. That's why this point gets front-row seating.

2. *Willingness to work overtime for the customer.* Your customer service representatives are so committed, they are, as the old rock-and-roll lyric goes, there when you need them. Keep this point close to the top so your readers can see and remember it.

3. *Thorough knowledge of service.* Obviously, knowledge means a lot. Yet, knowledge is different from problem solving. By positioning this point third down the line, and stepping into the shadows, you're putting the verbal spotlight where it belongs.

4. *Friendly manner on the telephone.* Yes, yes, yes, we're glad your representatives are friendly. And yes, yes, yes, we appreciate their phone manner. But come on . . . we're upset and want immediate answers. That's why this otherwise vital nicety belongs at the bottom of your list.

All pieces in place, your letter would look like this:

Dear _____ ,

We can help. Whether you're undergoing a routine procedure or emergency surgery, we'll make your health insurance experience easy so you can focus on recovering.

We do this by providing longer customer service hours than any health insurance company in the state—from 7:00 A.M. to 11:00 P.M. each weekday and from 9:00–5:00 on weekends. If your situation is unusually complex, our representatives will work overtime, contacting physicians and locating important documents until the process is complete. Need help other times? Just call our 24-hour hotline at 555-1212.

Regardless of when you contact us or why, you'll receive clear, comprehensive, and accurate information. Our representatives have at least five years of experience in numerous health insurance areas and regularly attend classes on everything from industry changes to spoken and written communication skills.

If you would like to know more, just call our office at 555-1213.

Sincerely,

Mary Ann Lonner
Manager, Customer Service Department

TRY THIS! Practice writing lists for letters or other documents that you consistently send to customers. Fiddle with each until you find one or two alternatives you like best. Then bring the lists to work and write the letters based on that order.

What's in a Look?

Perhaps you want a different kind of look for your list. For example, you may want to place each point on a single line. Although this style is more difficult to set up on the computer, some people prefer the visual effect. Let's say you're evaluating your sales department's manager. You'd probably write your list like this:

PAST SUCCESS	PRESENT SUCCESS			FUTURE SUCCESS
_____ +	_____ +	_____ +	_____ +	_____
New business	Corrects communications problems	Excellent presentations	Improves processes	Needs feedback to stay successful

As you can see, the top line is devoted to a general structure, while the bottom breaks the report into sections. The uppercase PAST, PRESENT, and FUTURE provides a quick visual connection between the end of the document and the beginning. Want to move points around? Some people cut and paste on the computer or simply ink in arrows:

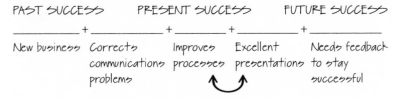

PAST SUCCESS	PRESENT SUCCESS			FUTURE SUCCESS
_____ +	_____ +	_____ +	_____ +	_____
New business	Corrects communications problems	Improves processes	Excellent presentations	Needs feedback to stay successful

You can also use columns for your list. This example includes details to guide your writing further:

Key points	Specifics
PAST SUCCESS	Employees closed 20 new accounts = $12 million
Corrects communications problems	Proposal rewrites
Improves processes	Strategies for new client
Excellent presentations	Provides objective data
FUTURE SUCCESS	Needs continued feedback

Regardless of your listing style or how many details you include, you'll ultimately create a report like that on page 19:

TRY THIS! Write a list for the following paragraph from this health club's brochure using a numerical list, a column, or any other order that's comfortable for you. Next reorder the list so it appeals to potential members who travel a lot. (Hint: You'd start with the National Stay Fit Club.) Then reorder it for those out-of-shape readers who want long-term benefits. Finally, write the paragraph anew.

> Why are Shape-Up Health Clubs better than those health clubs appearing at every corner? Start with money. Shape-Up will shave 25% off your membership through March 31. This entitles you to our complete workout facilities, including weight room, aerobics classes, and sauna. Of course, getting into shape is only as good as staying in shape. That's why our membership entitles you to become a member of the National Stay Fit Club. If you're traveling to a major city, chances are a member club will be just around the corner. Once there, just show your membership card and take a locker. All clubs, from Maine to Montana, open at 6:00 A.M. on weekdays and at 8:00 A.M. on weekends and stay open until 10:00 P.M.

Evaluation of Matthew Mannings

For the past year, Matthew Mannings has worked as a manager in our sales department. During that time, his employees have closed 20 new accounts totaling $12 million. The reasons for his success include his ability to determine the best strategies for winning customers and to

- *Correct communications problems.* Most recently, Matt identified soft spots in our proposals including old and irrelevant information. He then organized a team of five employees who revised the proposal and several other documents—without interrupting the regular work flow.

- *Analyze and improve his department's processes.* One of Matthew's greatest successes was identifying and incorporating new software so his employees could look at a potential customer's profile, isolate their areas of greatest concern, and develop a unique strategy for winning the account—in hours rather than days.

- *Give inspiring presentations to both customers and employees.* Matt's presentations move from one point to the next with an appropriate amount of objective information. In addition, he utilizes visuals such as charts and graphs to reinforce the information.

For Matt to continue with his rather impressive growth, he must stay conscious of changing trends in the industry and receive regular feedback from senior management. I am confident that he will pursue this course and continue to run a department whose sales exceed our expectations.

TEN DIFFERENT WAYS TO ORDER YOUR LIST

When listing, don't get caught in the drop-and-write trap. That's when every document has the same structure . . . again and again and again. You'll get bored, and you'll end up creating documents as

True or False

Establishing the most appropriate order will add time to your writing process.

False. Just review and choose one of the ten most common structural devices each time you write. Within a week or two, your mind will immediately click into the best order for your document and you won't need this list at all. Eventually you'll incorporate two or three different structures in every document, creating a truly sophisticated and convincing message. Stuck? Message stale? Return to these pages for a shot of inspiration or direction.

exciting as stale toast. Equally important, you'll miss a great opportunity to present your ideas in the most convincing way possible. To avoid this trap, pick from the following list of ten top orders or invent your own. You may want to mix several orders. If so, use transitions to take your readers from one to the next.

Ten Structure-Saving Orders

1. Most to least important
2. Equal importance
3. Least to most important
4. Directional
5. Chronological
6. Compare and contrast
7. Problem and solution
8. Question and answer
9. Cause and effect
10. True or false

When you write, be sure to use at least one of the ten top structure-saving orders and their transitions that you'll see on the following pages:

1. Most to Least Important

This is the most common order for virtually any document. Simply determine which points are the most intriguing and place them first. Save the less important points for later. That way, you stand a better chance of getting the impatient reader to absorb the essence of your message.

Warning: Never tell your readers that you're presenting the most important information first. If you do, why would they continue reading?

Use for

Response letters
Memos
Marketing letters
Newsletter articles
Reports
Employee evaluations
Proposals

Transitions include

First, second, third . . .
Also, in addition, finally . . .
One, two, three . . .
Bullets . . .

Look at this section from a security company's newsletter article:

While you're on vacation, avoid being prey to burglars. Lock all your doors and windows—including the ones in your basement and other easy-to-forget places. Also, arrange for a neighbor to pick up your mail and newspapers so your house looks occupied. Finally, keep a radio or even a television going. This may fool or intimidate many criminals.

2. Equal Importance

Here's another easy one, perfect for almost every kind of document and a cinch with bullets. Use this order when points are equally interesting and important.

Warning: When writing brochures, newsletters, and other documents with numerous sections, be careful not to overdose on this order. Since the transitions are pretty bland, you'll risk boring readers. A special hazard with bullets: more dots than a connect-the-dots puzzle.

Use for

Response letters
Memos
Sales and marketing materials
Reports
Proposals
Employee evaluations
Newsletter articles

Transitions include

One, two, three . . .
First, second, third . . .
In addition, also, finally . . .
Bullets

The following section is from a coffee-shop chain's information sheet:

So our customers can appreciate every drop, Coffees
International, Inc., does more than sell them coffee—we teach

them about the coffee-making processes. Our programs
include:

- Free coffee tastings with samples from Kenya, India, Costa
  Rica, and other countries
- Coffee-roasting demonstrations
- Films showing coffee bean harvests
- Demonstrations of the decaffeinating process
- Special discounts on our grinders, filters, and other coffee
  paraphernalia

3. Least to Most Important

This order is deceiving. After all, you *never* want to begin a piece
with a boring or unimpressive point. Yet you may have a list chock
full of interesting points with only slight degrees of greater importance. This is the perfect time to build suspense, moving the reader
from an important point to a *more* important point to the *most*
important point . . . much as a good story builds suspense into its
plot. And while you may not get oohs and ahs from your readers,
you increase the chances they will read from first line to last.

Use for

Response letters
Marketing and sales letters
Employee evaluations

Transitions include

Significant, more significant, of greatest significance . . .
More important, even more important, most important . . .
Furthermore, best of all . . .

Look at this section from a sales brochure:

Pure Water, Inc., has installed our special filter into over 60,000
kitchen sinks across the country, making families' tap water

cleaner and fresher tasting. Even more important, we've
installed our special Main Source Filtering System directly
into thousands of water tanks to ensure that every drop, in
bathroom sinks, showers, and even outdoor hoses, is as fresh
and healthy as possible. Most important, though, our customers
automatically join our Fresh Water Follow-up Plan to ensure that
their water maintains this superior quality for five years.

4. Directional

When discussing anything, from a beachside getaway to proper
behavior in a focus group, businesspeople mistakenly plop descriptions on the page, believing they'll somehow arrange themselves
into a cohesive order. Not true. Every description needs some sort of
logical movement that readers can follow as easily as a street map.
Depending on the document, you can move from left to right or
right to left; top to bottom or bottom to top; details to overview or
overview to details; and on and on. The main point: determine a
direction in your list and follow it.

Use with

Brochures
Reports
Manuals
Instructions

Transitions include

On the left, on the right ...
First, then, next ...
Top left, top right, travel to the bottom right ...
Close, even closer ...

Notice how this section from a brochure describing time-share
apartments in the Caribbean moves from an overview to specifics:

Envision a land where the temperature never dips below 75°
and never rises above 85°. Look closer and see a house tucked

into a mountainside overlooking a stark blue sea. Then, look
even closer and see an interior with a dishwasher, washing
machine, Jacuzzi, and every other modern convenience. Now,
imagine yourself living there two or even three months a year.

5. Chronological

Whenever possible, use this structure. It's easy for readers to follow. And it's easy to create, since it uses a clear, recognizable time
sequence.

Use for

Reports
Announcements for training sessions and events
Brochures publicizing events
Employee evaluations
Newsletter articles

Transitions include

First, then, next . . .
Hours—10:00, 11:00, 12:00 . . .
Days—Monday, Tuesday, Friday . . .
General time—This afternoon, by evening, the next day . . .

In this selection from a training manual announcing a course on
public speaking, notice how naturally the transitions fall:

> In the first two hours of this day-long seminar, you'll learn
> the ABC's of addressing audiences from the boardroom to
> the auditorium. In the second two-hour segment, you'll
> get valuable insights into what works and what doesn't
> work by watching and discussing film clips of well-known
> speakers, including Winston Churchill and Bill Clinton. After
> a complimentary lunch in the Chelsea Conference Room,
> you'll make a five-minute presentation, which you'll observe
> on video and discuss with a speech coach in the last hour of
> the afternoon.

6. Compare and Contrast

Remember this one from high school? When you compared and/or contrasted everything from novels to nations. In the business community, you can create a powerful and convincing document by comparing and contrasting products, services, employees, and opinions either line by line, paragraph by paragraph, or page by page.

You can compare from two to four or even five points. Don't worry about allotting equal space to each; just include credible, in-depth information.

Use for

Response letters
Pitch letters
Press releases
Letters to the editor
Sales materials

Transitions include

On the one hand, on the other hand . . .
However . . .
Similarly, in contrast . . .
Actually . . .
The truth is . . .

The following letter to the editor of a large city newspaper is a classic example of contrasting points. Here, the transitions focus on the truth—or lack of truth—in the previous point:

> In your June 19 article you stated that our nightclub has a policy prohibiting women from walking through our doors. This is perfectly untrue. Rather, we welcome women and frequently have "girls' night out," a woman-only event with live bands and free admission. You also wrongly stated that we use scare tactics such as hostile looks or suggestive comments to keep women away. In fact, we have instructed all our doormen to escort

women to and from their cars so they'll feel especially comfortable spending an evening here. Finally, you stated that we prohibit women from executive positions within the corporation. Again, untrue! Our president is a woman!

7. Problem and Solution

As the old adage goes, the proof is in the pudding. And a problem–solution structure is the richest, most reassuring type of pudding anywhere. With this order, you're doing more than making promises about your wonderful product, service, or employee— you're giving evidence of your success. And, problem–solution structures are anecdotal—always a plus in any type of business writing.

Use for

Response letters
Sales and marketing materials
Reports

Transitions include

Problem: . . . Solution: . . .
Here was the problem: . . . This was our solution: . . .
How can? This is how . . .

This client's information sheet opens by establishing tension, which the next paragraph resolves:

Problem: A wave of cars waited 20 minutes to leave an urban parking garage at rush hour every day. How, the owners asked, could they move traffic faster without changing the physical layout of the garage?

Solution: We set up a station on the ground floor so drivers can pay their fees before getting in their cars.

Problem: A business community suffered from limited parking. Worse, the students at a nearby college were taking up most

of the spaces in front of stores. The college didn't have room
for another parking lot. The business community was fed up.
How could they end the friction?

Solution: We arranged for public transportation to shuttle
students to campus from a parking lot across town.

This piece then explained that the company found such fast and
feasible solutions thanks to its well-educated staff and dynamic
group approach to every problem.

8. Question and Answer

Businesspeople love using questions and answers in their documents. This format is compelling—when you provide a question,
your readers hunger for an answer. And creating a list in this order
is relatively easy. Beware, though, of the quicksand sucking in all
good Q&A intentions—boring questions followed by blasé answers.
Also, be sure to weave your Q&A's together with a strong narrative
or your piece will fall apart.

Use for

Response letters
Sales and marketing materials
Manuals
Instruction sheets

Transitions include

Question: . . . Answer: . . .
Yes, . . . or No, . . .

Notice the specific answers in this section from a response letter:

Thank you for inquiring about franchising opportunities at
Bright Day Child Care. The following will provide you with
answers to prospective owners most common questions:

Do you subscribe to one method of child care?

Yes. We follow the methods of Richard Clark, a well-known, London-based child psychologist and educator.

Must teachers have special training or degrees?

Yes. We prefer that our teachers have a master's, or at least a bachelor's degree, in early childhood education. At a minimum, they must have at least two years of formal training and at least five years' experience in day-care centers, nursery schools, or other organized settings.

9. Cause and Effect

Establishing a cause-and-effect structure is one surefire way to resolve disputes, answer questions, soothe doubts. Simply structure your piece by showing an action and then the resulting reaction. Whenever possible, be objective, relying on what your readers could or did see, feel, hear, or smell.

Use with

Reports
Information sheets
Articles for professional publications and newsletters
Employee evaluations
Response letters

Transitions include

As a result . . .
First, next, then . . .

Here's a typical cause-and-effect letter telling a customer how a harmless, although upsetting, situation occurred:

Thank you for contacting us about your Toast Plus Kitchen Master. We have located the source of your problem. It seems

as though a piece of plastic—probably from a plastic bag—
got lodged in the heating coil. When you turned the machine
on, the plastic started smoking and created an unpleasant odor.
Please note: the machine could not have exploded or in any
way jeopardized the health of you or your family.

10. True or False

This structural device is reserved primarily for catchy marketing
materials. The setup is gamelike, inviting the reader to participate by
guessing whether the statement is true or false. Since all great
devices wither with use, use this structure for only a page or two.

Use with

Marketing letters and brochures
Newsletter articles
Informational material

Transitions include

True or false? True, ... [or False, ...]

In this sample from an automobile insurance company newsletter, the reader is compelled not only to *read* but to *think* about the
message:

Test your safety know-how by answering these true or false
questions:

True or false? Air bags are 100% effective in preventing injuries
due to accidents.

False. While air bags do cut down the number of deaths and
injuries, they are not completely effective. In fact, they can
even cause injuries.

True or false? Air bags can open at a rate of 100 miles per hour.

True. Air bags are exceedingly fast, which can be dangerous to
infants and elderly passengers.

TRY THIS! Each of these paragraphs contains one or more structural devices. Identify them, then revise the paragraph using different options.

1. Through the years, The Thompson School graduates have returned to our halls and classrooms for visits. They recall their first day in the new school: their curiosity, their excitement, their fear. They tell us about how they gradually adjusted as they became more deeply involved in the classroom and extracurricular experiences. And, of course, they remember with some sadness the day, four years later, when they graduated. As they left our doors, though, they carried numerous advantages. They had a solid foundation in reading, writing, math, and other core skills. More important, they could apply these skills to everyday challenges. Most important, though, they had the self-confidence to create a life that would allow them and their new families to grow and flourish.

2. Like businesses everywhere, you have a problem: your overhead is threatening to exceed your profits. And we have a solution: our exclusive Print Program. Within the first year of using our program, your organization will save a full 15% on your current costs for printed materials. Chances are, you have a second problem, too: your staff is tied up with too many details and not enough time to address them all. Our Print Program is hassle-free because we do all the work in these three steps:

    A. Analysis and Design. We'll develop a comprehensive plan covering everything from the most competitively priced design of your materials to the most efficient storage and distribution system.

    B. Storage. So you have more warehouse space, we'll store your materials *free of charge,* and deliver the

material where you want and when you want it with
only four hours' notice.

C. Regular updates. With our computerized system, we'll
update you as to how much material you've used, how
much you have in stock, and what's given you the
greatest return for your investment.

3. To ensure a comfortable, homey environment, always greet
new arrivals by name and ask how they are feeling. If you
notice someone having a hard time on the machines or
searching for the right locker, offer to help. Be sure to keep
the club clean, too. If you notice a spill, litter, or wet towel on
the floor, pick it up. If a member complains about a dirty sink
or shower, check the situation yourself; then, if the problem
is complicated, call the janitorial service listed in the main
office. Most important though, create a safe environment.
If you see that a member has poor posture when lifting
weights, correct it. If a member is using free weights that
are too heavy, suggest a change. These details can mean
the difference between a satisfied member and an injured
one.

TRY THIS, too. Write down each point from one or two letters or
other short documents you have recently written. Then, rearrange
that list, placing your information in two or three different orders.
Be clear about why you have structured your list each way.

PUTTING UP THE WRITING UMBRELLA

In addition to using a cohesive structure, you can create an intricate
design from first line to last by placing your message under a idea
umbrella. Before or after you write your list, find a *metaphor* to

weave throughout the document or an *anecdote* to refer to several times. Then, on your list, show how the umbrella idea connects to several or all of your points. This works particularly well with training and sales and marketing materials and instructions.

Let's look more closely at umbrella ideas, starting with metaphors and similes—those wonderful devices you probably recall from English class.

Metaphors and Similes

Perhaps the most popular metaphor ever is "Love is a rose". Love, of course, isn't a rose, but the image conjures both beauty and pain, which, in this era of instant marriage and rampant divorce is pretty accurate.

In business writing you are likely to encounter metaphors and similes such as these:

> Our mattress is a soft cloud floating you off to sleep.

> Today's economy is like a cobra waiting to strike.

Regardless of which you use, metaphors and similes create better documents.

> *Without metaphor:* To avoid backlog that hurts our organization, don't let papers collect on your desk.

> *With metaphor:* Papers collecting on your desk are like rust corroding our organization.

The reasons for their effectiveness, however, run deeper than you might think. Here are some:

• *Image.* By using a cloud, cobra, or any other vivid image, you give readers an effective way to remember your message. Think about the advertisements you see on television, on billboards, or in magazines. Whether the ads feature Calvin Klein's controversial nymphets or Coors's mountain scenes, you recall the picture even before the product name.

- *Association.* Whenever you write, your mission is the same: to involve your readers as directly and completely as possible. By using metaphors and similes you allow the readers to associate their own experiences, memories, or connotations.

- *Interesting language.* Regardless of the image, you're bound to use unusual—and refreshing—language with metaphors and similes. This will help distinguish your message from others, and in the process will interest the reader.

Warning: Avoid using tired metaphors and similes such as these from an MIS department:

> Using new technology can be like drowning in quicksand. That's why all employees should attend the computer training sessions every Thursday afternoon in the McNeil Conference Room.

> In the software battlefield, developers must fight many battles before winning the war.

Even readers whose knowledge of the written word comes from cereal boxes are familiar with metaphors using battlefields and quicksand. Those images are flat. Strong alternatives include:

> Using new technology can be like following a complicated road map. Rather than lose your way, attend the computer training sessions. . . .

> In the software competition, developers must play for many innings before winning the game. The first, and most critical, round is with the marketability of their products.

However, be careful of creating self-conscious metaphors and similes. For example, this line will certainly overwhelm the reader:

> Every customer is like a long-lost relative visiting from the Far East.

Instead, keep it simple and write:

> Every customer is like a visiting relative.

Or, more simply:

>Every customer is like family.

Now, take a look at the following list and the press release a PR writer created from it:

1. Business must dress nicely—compare to well-dressed person
2. Tips for results—image out of closet
3. Sessions
4. Bio and prices—runway for success

For: Imaging Consultants
16 West Street, Cranston, NY 20012

Contact: John Phillips 555-4321

FOR IMMEDIATE RELEASE

Imaging Consultants Show Businesses How to Really Dress

Cranston, NY, May 19, 1998 — Business owners aren't the only ones who have to dress nicely—their businesses do too. That's why, in this two-day conference at Hiner's Center in the downtown financial district, Imaging Consultants is showing entrepreneurs how to transform underdressed offices into tailored workplaces.

"We're trying to show small business owners how to take image out of the closet and into the workplace," says Imaging Consultants trainer Sue Reed. "We give them valuable tips about how to maximize office space to accommodate more employees, use color to make clients feel comfortable, and pick furniture that is comfortable, functional, and professional."

Some of the sessions include "Finding Your Own Image," "Improving the Office Step-by-Step," and "Behind the Walls—Creating Productive Space." Participants receive handouts, charts, before-and-after samples, and other materials. They are also encouraged to bring photos of their offices for complimentary sessions with Imaging Consultants' staff.

Imaging Consultants has been helping businesses walk the runway to success for over a decade. Its clients include Stonewall Bank, The Chamber of Commerce, The Business Center Supply Company, and other local and regional organizations. Says Imaging Consultants president Jon Woo: "We don't believe business owners need to dig up loans so they can have a professional-looking office. All our events and services are geared to help clients look good through financially sensible choices and not outrageously high prices."

Individuals interested in Imaging Consultants' conference can receive more information by calling 555-666-6666.

Instant Metaphors

Use these as metaphors in your message:

A penguin waddling on ice
The Charleston
A watch with a second hand doing double-time
Play clay
A cold cup of coffee
A yowling cat
A bent paper clip
A leaky house
Lukewarm water
The Tour de France
A motorcycle with two flat tires
A children's book
A nuclear device

Poison ivy
A computer virus
A yellow sports car
Summer camp
Wet paint
A tapeworm
An ice cream cone on a hot day
A long weekend
Corn on the cob
A bucket of ice
Tight shoes
A quiver of arrows
Last week's bread
A room full of three-year olds

TRY THIS! Using the chart that follows, list a topic you write about every day, such as a product name, an idea, or a service that is important to your organization. Then write an outstanding characteristic—a physical attribute, a result it brings, or an unusual feature. Next think of an object, any object, that shares that characteristic and create your metaphor. Don't like your object? Think it's cliché? Then write several others until you find one that works.

Topic	Characteristic	Object with similar characteristic	Metaphor
Investments	Challenging	Chess game	Investing is like playing chess: you must strategize every move
Phone calls	Frequent	Snow in Alaska	The phone rings as predictably as snow falls in Alaska

Anecdotes

Everybody loves a good story—those chronological accounts that have a beginning, a middle, and an end, with some sort of impressive outcome. Step into any bar, dinner party, or everyday telephone conversation and that's what you'll hear. Writing for business, you've probably used stories in bios and case histories. But don't be limited. Stories are great for all types of documents, from information sheets to faxed memos.

Say you're writing sales and marketing materials—simply give the reader a chronological account of how your business's service or product has helped a customer. When dealing with complaint letters, review the situation from the customer's point of view. Then, in the following paragraphs, keep referring to the story. This will help you support your claims, create continuity within the document, and use interesting language and ideas. Just make sure your story has the following elements:

- *Interesting events.* Make sure the story is absorbing. With sales and marketing material, for example, make sure something is at stake, such as the customer's financial gain, physical well-being, or emotional security.

- *Specific information.* To make your story as vivid as possible, include details such as names, dollar amounts, and ages when relevant.

- *Typical scenario.* Stick with scenes your reader can relate to. Discussing financial services? Mention the average client rather than an extremely wealthy one—unless you helped him or her get that way. Discussing your catering business? Mention weddings and bar mitzvahs that may be similar to those your reader would host.

Now, look at this example from one company's annual report:

> Tommy James has had asthma since the day he was born. While asthma is troublesome, Tommy's case was even more serious—his brother, Sam, had died from asthma two years before. During Tommy's most recent bout, his mother contacted our Medical Hotline. In addition to telling her to drive Tommy to the emergency ward immediately, our medical emergency specialist explained that Tommy should remain calm and limit his use of the inhaler. Then, our specialist contacted the hospital to alert the doctors of Tommy's arrival.

Typically, you'd refer to your anecdote in two ways:

1. At the beginning of your document to establish a scene; in the middle, to remind your readers and create a consistent structure; and at the end, so you can tie the whole piece together.

2. Each time you mention a new or especially important point, to support your statements and create continuity.

The Tommy James example continues:

> We make sure our medical emergency specialists give only
> the best advice to people like Tommy's mother by using
> only experienced nurses. They regularly attend college
> courses so they're updated about the newest advances in
> everything from cancer treatments to asthma. In addition,
> they're trained communicators who give callers information
> clearly and directly. This especially helps distressed callers,
> like Tommy's mother, react in the most levelheaded, effective
> way.

TROUBLESHOOTING

Think listing's a problem? Don't be fooled. Just because you feel too rushed to list, forget to list, or simply don't *want* to list, don't ignore this important step. Instead, revitalize your commitment to writing well and remind yourself that in the end, listing saves more time than it takes. Still, listing isn't for everyone. Here are some indications it isn't for you.

Writing problems. Perhaps the words drip slowly, and it takes 15 minutes, half an hour, an hour to write only a few paragraphs. Or perhaps the information never reaches the page. If listing doesn't speed up your writing process and help orient you, it's not working.

Scattered or vanishing points. If the latest mystery in your life is what points to include in your document, better pause before drawing up your next list. Similarly, if you spend your writing time trying to recall those wonderful details, examples, and other support points that bloomed fresh as summer daisies in your mind just moments before you sat at the computer, forget about listing.

Frustration when trying to determine your points. The principle behind listing is that the ideas you want to write are already in your head. The order may be askew, the essence half-formed, but the ideas *are* there. By listing, you allow them to tumble onto the page from their captivity within your mind. If the ideas don't tumble, but plod or shift restlessly, then try something else.

To List or Not to List

I once had a client who earned an enviably lucrative living creating in-depth reports and proposals for a successful international corporation. Then something terrible occurred: he couldn't write. Simply put, he was blocked. And though he struggled, took the advice of countless colleagues, tried every exercise in every self-help book in every bookstore, the words remained wedged inside.

When he came to my office for help, I asked about his writing process. "Well," he said, "I gather my information, then start writing."

"Do you use an outline?" I asked.

He shook his head and confessed that he, like most people in the business world, simply placed fingers to computer keys and got to work. Naturally, I advised him to write a quick list and organize his points before he started writing. That way he'd have a stronger sense of direction and would have an easier time transitioning into the text.

He tried, but returned the next week equally distressed. "When exactly does your block begin?" I asked.

He sighed, sipped from a paper cup of lukewarm coffee, and said, "With the first word. Before that, when I have to gather information or interview people, I'm fine. But I just can't seem to write."

"When was your best writing experience?" I asked, hoping to find some clues there.

He thought a moment, sipped his coffee, thought a little more. At last he said, "In college I had a professor who made us outline every idea before we wrote. We even had to use index cards. It was the best writing experience I ever had."

"Then why did you stop writing that way?"

"I guess because it seemed to take too long. In fact, when I started getting blocked, everyone told me to relax and let the words flow even faster."

Obviously, the words didn't flow for him. They jelled and clotted. Even a list didn't help. Ultimately, my client had to recognize his own process and yield graciously, even willingly, to its demands. He started his process by organizing his material, then wrote his ideas in a detailed stream-of-consciousness type of list, then, finally, wrote. In the end, my client wasn't the fastest writer in the department. But he did manage to get the kinks out of his own process and write faster than he did in college and, most important, avoid additional blocks.

So, what are the best alternatives to listing? Here are the two most popular ones.

Outlining

Sometimes, such as when you're writing a complicated proposal or white paper, the light that listing provides won't be enough. You'll need an outline that reveals every point and subpoint along the way. First, though, consider these pros and cons:

Pro: Outlines can help you arrange your points in the most orderly, logical way before you even begin paragraph one.

Pro: Outlines take the tension out of writing by providing a clear, definite direction.

Pro: With outlines, you have more control over your word use because you know precisely when you've completed one idea and should move on to another.

Pro: Outlines can cut your writing time by helping you organize your thoughts to the last detail.

Con: By fitting too much information into a mold, outlines can make the writing process mechanical, even boring.

Con: Frequently, especially with reports and research papers, you won't know exactly what you want to say until you say it.

Con: Outlines can make word use dry because they inhibit creativity.

Con: Outlines can lengthen your writing time because they take so long to create.

Freewriting

Many writing coaches and seminar leaders extol the virtues of freewriting. They reason, if you have something to say, you should say it. That's all. Don't plot, plan, or break down your thoughts. "Loosen up," they say, "and the words will flow like spring rain."

These writing experts are reacting, in part, to the processing plant of our education, which taught us to plan, plan, plan everything from the opening and the closing lines of *each* paragraph to the least significant punctuation mark. They're right, too. Most of us do need to loosen up and forget the constraints our education placed on us. We need to flow. The trouble with flowing, of course, is that you can flow miles away from your main points and never come back. However, if you do feel more comfortable freewriting, go ahead. But— and this is a big *but*—as you go, take a second or two and list your main thoughts as you write them. Then you'll have a quick and easy way to track your thoughts when you rewrite.

CONCLUSION

The first step to writing should be listing the points you want to make. In whatever order they come out. In whatever format you prefer. Once you have those points on paper, you can arrange them for maximum effect and open a lively writing umbrealla over them. Then ... start writing!

Writing

Object: *To write your message quickly and easily—without frustrating pauses or blocks. Average time for a double-spaced page: five to ten minutes.*

Now that you have your list, the next step is the most obvious and inevitable: writing. Ideally, writing should be as simple as sipping a soda, the scene at your office looking something like this:

> You sit at your desk, computer keyboard or pad of paper before you. You start writing. The first few words flow easily; the ones that follow, even more so. You consult your list as you move along, reminding yourself of otherwise lost points, spontaneously adding extra examples or support. Within five or ten minutes you've finished your letter or memo. Within an hour or two you've breezed through several pages of your proposal or report. Yes, you think to yourself, you'll make your deadline, no problem.

The sad reality is that most people find that their words drip or stumble onto the computer screen. When describing their feelings about writing, my clients have used such words as agonizing, excruciating, and torturous. Rather than create fresh copy, others have confessed to ignoring important letters, sending a colleague's dubious proposal, and using forms that were seriously outdated. Even if you are an avoidance junkie and have an impressive set of your own confessions, you know that you can't escape writing altogether.

Unfortunately, your feelings about writing interfere with your ability to write. Why? When you hate doing something you grow tense when doing it. Think about driving in traffic. Chances are your stomach gets knotted and you feel distracted, restless, impatient. Perhaps you shout epithets that would make Quentin Tarantino blush. When writing, you probably experience the same anxieties, ranging from irritation to frustration to outrage. And while you may not swear or shout aloud, your writing slows, words dropping stiff and stilted. The more you struggle, the slower the words flow, the stiffer they get. Naturally, this experience adds to your dread the inevitable next time you must create that letter, report, or E-mail message.

Perhaps you, like many people, invent excuses—albeit groundless excuses—about why writing really isn't important.

The Businessperson's Most Popular Excuses for Not Writing Carefully

1. No one reads business writing.
2. No one reads beyond the first paragraph.
3. Our readers only look at dollar signs.
4. Graphs are much more important.
5. Our telephone conversations cement our client relationships.
6. We should put time into more important things.
7. We should put energy only into our strengths—and writing isn't one of mine.
8. Our readers receive too much written material anyway—why add more?
9. The marketing department writes the really important pieces. Ours don't really matter.
10. Our readers know what they think. Writing to them won't help either way.

Excuses give you license to lunge through the writing stage, calling up old letters and signing your name, writing without a list, writing without planning to rewrite.

The obvious solution to this word-wilting dilemma is to relax. Yet, as the old adage goes: Easier said than done. Much easier. The truth is, though, that you *can* relax and the words *can* flow and, yes, you *can* enjoy writing. Really. The best place to start is with a look at why you hate writing.

DARK SHADOWS: THE GHOSTS HAUNTING YOUR WRITING PROCESS

You go to a friend's swimming pool. You swim a few laps, lie in the sun, eat a burger. The experience is enjoyable and relaxing. You have some associations connected with this event, all generally positive. Now, compare this to writing. You go to your office, sit at the computer, start to write, and BAM! A barrage of ghosts wearing combat boots and carrying clubs surface from your subconscious.

Perhaps you don't feel these sensations on a conscious level. But be assured, most people carry more writing-related baggage than a mail carrier does letters. That's because writing speaks a great deal about the person you *are*, in addition to the thoughts you are trying to project.

Take intelligence. People have always had prejudices about the intelligence and overall sophistication of others based on their word use—whether spoken, written, or tapped in Morse code. Movies, books, and television shows from Saturday morning cartoons to Martin Scorsese movies depict people with poor grammar as crude, dim-witted thugs, inbred hillbillies, or general lowlifes. These people say things such as:

I don't got no job so I ain't got no money.

instead of the more grammatical:

I don't have a job, so I don't have any money.

In high school, the smart people received A's on history and social science essays, soaring on the academic crest with their finessed

English papers. You may have been one of these expert writers, or you may have been intelligent in different ways. Perhaps you excelled in theater classes, acting out Shakespeare with unflinching ease. Perhaps you tore apart a car engine and reassembled it in moments flat. Inadvertently or not, the powers that be determined that so-so writers had only so-so intelligence.

High School and College Education

Generally, our teachers were good people, underpaid and overly devoted. Some of them were plainly inspirational. One good example is my high school teacher Donald Rawding. A small, thin man with soft, sincere mannerisms, he persuaded us to drop our sarcastic veneer and sincerely, openly express ourselves. He used all the right tools, too: journal writing, freewriting assignments, and plenty of feedback in his scrawled hand. Most of his comments were positive, some of them negative, all of them honest. Almost 25 years after having Donald Rawding as my teacher, I clearly recognize his impact on my choice to become a professional writer.

Many of your teachers were like Donald Rawding. Yet you probably recall many others who inadvertently knit a fabric of dread that still tightens around you 10, 20, 30, or more years after you have shed cap and gown. Their fabric typically included the following three components.

Inappropriate teaching methods

When you were a student, your young mind probably burned with ideas, opinions, and information. Yet your education most likely smoldered this flame with grammar rules and instructions on how to diagram sentences and distinguish a gerund from a participle. In the process, you started thinking that writing was as clear-cut as math, where one and one make two no matter how many times you toy with the numbers. In reality, writing is never black-and-white. It's full of endless shades of gray and flamboyant colors that no rules can completely control.

TRY THIS! Saying So Long to Your Teacher. Write a paragraph about a teacher who inhibited your writing skill. Perhaps this person was a college professor who assigned absurd papers—and too many of them. Perhaps he or she was a junior high school teacher who once commented that your writing skills were far below average. Explain exactly how that teacher affected you.

Then, write a paragraph about a teacher who fostered your abilities, making you feel confident enough to overcome any obstacle, with writing or in another way. Whenever you have trouble writing, take a few moments to recall that second teacher and all the positive thoughts and feelings he or she inspired. Finally, visualize that teacher escorting the first one out of your life.

Remember, *don't* worry about your writing style in this exercise. Your mission is simply to get the words out.

Here is a client's sample:

> I can never forget my junior high school teacher Miss O'Malley: a classic 1960s bombshell with a jet-black bouffant hairdo, tight dress, spike heels, and plenty of makeup, who dated, naturally enough, the gym teacher. Miss O'Malley was quiet and shy but had a fierce red pen. Her main concern was grammar, diagramming sentences, that sort of thing. Up until that point, I loved to write. But after getting low grades on my quizzes and papers—and a C in the class—I had a hard time. That feeling still lingers.
>
> On the other hand, I had a great drama teacher in high school. He doubled as an art teacher and his wife taught English, although not my class. Both of them believed in me. They gave me the best role in the school play, spent time talking to me about my other classes, gave me suggestions on papers for other classes before I passed them in. More importantly, they liked me. In fact, they once invited me and a few of my friends for dinner at their house. From them, I learned that I was smart, creative, and capable.

Red-letter comments

Each teacher had his or her own method of commenting—little checks, dots, circles, and, of course, glaring X's, all denoting failure or success. As you moved from school essays to business letters, those red-letter comments cast a faint but unpleasant shadow that caused you to double-check your thoughts, rewrite prematurely and basically, and slow down your writing. This response is so universal that everyone, from editors to writing coaches, learns to write comments in blue, black, even green—but not red. The very color intimidates the businessperson beyond receptivity.

Grades

Perhaps the most intimidating factor in your entire educational experience was those letter grades at the top or the back of your papers telling you three things: (1) how you measured against some seemingly arbitrary standard of writing—which either a teacher or a textbook determined; (2) whether you were an abject failure or budding success; and (3) reminding you, however falsely, that your writing would forever be judged not by its merits as a communication device but as a test of your ability to follow rules.

As an adult, you know that self-consciousness only inhibits your ability to perform well. Like a dancer, you have complete control when you lose control and let out your true forms of self-expression. When you feel you're being judged, you become awkward, your steps out of beat. When writing, you have the same calamitous experience: the words don't seem to come, and when they do, they're as delicate as a garbage truck.

Unwelcome Editor

Each time you sit to write, an editor finds a place nearby, complaining because your sentences are too long, your word choice too simple, the information all wrong. Sometimes this editor sits on your shoulder, desktop, or computer stand, his or her loud voice camou-

flaged as your own. You listen and respond, rewriting a word, paragraph, or line again and again. With each revision, the editor whines:
"Nope, that one's as bad as the last." Or sometimes the editor speaks
from your subconscious, wordlessly criticizing you at every turn,
causing you to pause, rewrite, think, rewrite, and, against the hope-
lessness of it all, grow distracted.

The editor can be one, or even two or more, people. Perhaps these
people never saw your writing, never even discussed it. Perhaps they
did. Most important, their impact rests on how they made you feel
about yourself. Here are a few of the editors my clients and associates have told me about:

- *Parents.* Although parents undoubtedly affect their children in
  positive, life-sustaining ways, they can also be the most vocal and
  constant editors. Perhaps your parents' expectations were too
  high—they wanted you to get A's when you got B$^+$'s or to get A$^+$'s
  when you got A's. Perhaps they compared you to their friends'
  children, telling you openly or discreetly that you didn't measure
  up. Or maybe they disapproved of or were indifferent to your best
  efforts. Whatever the case, they appear as your editors, critically
  watching as you struggle to make your point.

- *Siblings.* The sibling-as-editor has two forms. First is the sibling
  who received better grades and won the teacher's approval year
  after year. You had to traipse along in your sibling's wake, trying
  unsuccessfully to be as clever and bright, or watch from afar as
  your illustrious sibling won every award, acknowledgment, and
  accolade. Or, you were the bright one, whom your siblings watched
  with admiration and dismay. As a grown-up, you have to keep up
  the momentum, although you long to limp along the lane of com-
  placency, for a short while anyway. Your watchful siblings are the
  editors perched on your lamp shade, magnifying glasses poised to
  catch your mistakes.

- *Teachers.* The most obvious editor was also probably your first—
  a teacher. But don't assume that English teachers are the ones who

lurk nearby. Perhaps you had a coach who pounded you with negative messages. Or a math or science teacher who made inappropriate comments throughout the year. Their voices stuck, one octave above all the others you've heard throughout your life.

- *Bosses.* The editor who creates the greatest confusion among businesspeople is the boss-as-editor. After all, most people in senior-level positions know how to manage and are experts on the company's products and services. But—and this is a big but—are

---

TRY THIS! Silencing the Editor. In one or two paragraphs, describe the editor who sits on your back or looms in the far reaches of your mind. Then, in the next paragraph, explain why you don't need that editor. Keep this piece of paper with you. Every time you get blocked, feel your writing plunking rather than flowing onto the page, or feel frustration rising like a fever, read this paper. After a week or two you should write more freely. After a month, the editor should have moved away.

Here is an example from a client:

> **Editor:** Without a doubt, my editor is my older brother, Roy. When we were growing up, he always did better than I at just about everything—he was a better basketball player and a better student, and he was more popular at school. Even now, I feel diminished by him.

> **Response:** Roy and I have grown into very separate people with our own types of success. My job running a multimedia facility requires ingenuity and brains. When I have challenges, I overcome them. One example is our bid for the Lytronics job. Thanks in large part to my presentation—which I had to complete in less than two days—we got this million-dollar client. Roy's position as vice president of RKE Development is important, but so is mine.

---

they really editors? The answer is usually an equally big no! Chances are you've had—or still have—a boss who ruthlessly rewrote your documents or insisted that you make vague and confusing changes. You complied, your boss's critical voice resonating over the years until it snuggled into your process, as persistent and annoying as a cockroach, even years later.

- *Arbitrary criteria.* As a child, you probably imagined the ideal person you wanted to be. Your ideas sprang from numerous sources: Barbie and Ken dolls, Superman comic books, and television shows ranging from *Ed Sullivan* to *Mr. Ed*. Mostly, though, you created an ideal self based on arbitrary standards that you gathered from your family, school, culture, and friends. Similarly, your internal editor insists that you create documents based on equally arbitrary and unattainable standards. It tells you that your opening paragraph isn't fast enough, your voice isn't friendly enough, and that proposal is nowhere near convincing enough.

READY TO WRITE

Type, Write or Dictate . . . ?

By now, everyone in the business world from Mississippi to Maine knows that communications are going electronic. Sometime soon, businesspeople will write exclusively on computers. Until then, however, the question still arises, Which is better: keyboard, pen, or dictation?

Most likely, you'll find the answer at work. I'm always amazed at how many of my corporate clients don't supply their employees with computers. Instead, they write letters by hand and send them to secretaries who diligently type away. Or, they dictate their messages which secretaries type and mail. Other clients insist that their employees type every word on the computer, whether it is a quick memo or a lengthy report. Some corporations have employees send documents electronically so that their message never actually moves from screen to paper.

When you do have a choice, which of the three forms of writing is best? For most people, the computer is the first choice. But each form has both drawbacks and advantages.

Computer

Pros: The computer is the businessperson's jet, while pen and dictation are twin-engine planes teetering tentatively in the breeze. With computers you can write quickly, letting your fingers fly from key to key. Make a mistake? Just backspace and delete. Need to add a point three lines up? Just move the cursor and type away. One of the greatest advantages of the computer is that if you save your writing periodically, on floppy as well as hard disk, you can easily file your work. Finally, computers are the future. Already businesspeople E-mail internal and external messages of every length, bypassing the days of ink and paper altogether.

Cons: As a former computerphobe I can tell you that the downside of computers is shrinking as the benefits rise. Still, here it is:

1. Computers are expensive. A good computer can cost between $1,000 and $10,000. That's a lot compared with the few hundred dollars you'd spend on a typewriter and the $3 you'd spend every few months on paper and pen.

2. Once you save enough to buy that computer or your company gives you one, you must learn to use it.

3. Computers can cause health problems, such as bad backs, headaches, and carpal tunnel syndrome, if your chair and the screen aren't positioned right.

Pen

Pros: Except for personal letters, handwritten notes are withering into extinction. But, yes, pen and paper do have advantages. This mode of writing is familiar, particularly if you grew up writing longhand. Besides, a pad of paper is infinitely easier to carry around than even the smallest, most lightweight computer. Just slip it in your bag or briefcase. Smash it into a wall? It's all right; paper doesn't break. Damage the pad? Don't worry about the expense of repairs; just purchase another. Some people like the feel of writing; the movement of their hands against the paper somehow brings the message closer.

Cons: Writing with pen and paper is perhaps one of the greatest time wasters in the business world. For starters, you need to duplicate your effort; you write, then input what you have written into the computer or typewriter. Make a mistake? You need to scratch out your words, creating an inky mess. Finally, handwritten documents are hard to organize, particularly if you bring work home from the office.

Dictation

Pros: Surprise! People actually do dictate. Perhaps you're one of them. And although many people claim that dictation is best suited for *Perry Mason* reruns, dictation does have some benefits. First, it's the fastest way to get your message out—fastest for the dictator, that is. In addition, you can dictate anywhere—in the car as you rush between appointments, in a restaurant while waiting for a client, in bed as you doze off to sleep. And, you can dictate with your eyes closed.

Cons: Dictation ravenously consumes massive amounts of time. You dictate the message, then another person has to type it, winding and rewinding the tape to catch particularly complex portions. If you're sending the message, you have very little editorial control. When speaking, you can't see the words, and you really have no idea how they translate as a written message. You have to hope that the person transcribing your words is a strong writer and can give them the shape and sense they need. Finally, unlike writing, which gives you maximum contact with words, dictating won't help you communicate better. Your words just drift onto a machine and ultimately . . . away.

Warming Up or Starting Cold

Think of basketball players. Before they start down the court to meet the opposition, they warm up. Their exercises consist of moves from running, to shooting the ball, to dribbling across court. Some businesspeople need writing warm-ups to get their fingers nimble, loosen the words, and stir up the fire of ideas.

When Will Warming Up Enhance Your Writing Process?

Sign: Typically, you get stuck while writing your document, falter through the opening paragraph, or spend a half hour or more on a one-page letter or memo. Or perhaps you feel anxious about writing or feel restless the moment you conjure that first word. If so, always warm up. This will diffuse your nervous energy and condition you to have a more relaxed response the next time you write.

Sign: Usually you have no trouble writing. But sometimes you feel unusually stressed or distracted, whether because the document you're writing makes taxes look fun, or the day's just overall horrendous. Warming up will alleviate the tension and ground your thoughts. Try warming up when you must write particularly difficult projects—it will open the word-use channels.

You're probably thinking that warming up is a luxury for those who have inherited gobs of time while you must pilfer every spare second. But warm-ups really are time efficient, even when letters pile up on your desk, the phone rings nonstop, and your voice mail is full. Here are a few ways to warm up without slowing down your workday:

- **Read a newspaper or a magazine over morning coffee or on the train to work.** Perhaps the most overlooked and underestimated way to oil your writing joints is through reading. Just open the magazine of your choice—whether *Sports Illustrated* or *The New Yorker*—and indulge. A few pointers: First, be sure the magazine's word use is relaxed and the style similar to yours. Reading a terse or weighty document will inhibit, rather than encourage, word flow. Next, read regularly every morning, at the same time if possible. Pick the most natural time—when you'd normally be sipping coffee or relaxing on the commuter train. Finally, read something you *enjoy*. Sound obvious? People often approach writing like medicine, believing that the most unpleasant-tasting doses are the most helpful. Not true. By reading material you enjoy, you'll read more closely, be more aware of the writing style, and read more often.

- **Create lists for several documents at once.** This warm-up technique is useful only if you have two or three documents to write that day. You may have to write several letters, a letter and two reports, or two sections of a proposal. Spend a little time creating lists for each item you must write. This process will help you channel your thoughts, work out your ideas, and loosen up for the actual writing. It will also help you determine a schedule, so you're sure to make every deadline.

- **Write letters and short communications.** Another great way to warm up is to save the more difficult documents for last. This is not a procrastination trick. By spending time on the easier, and often shorter, documents, you're warming up for the tasks to come. Fiction writers use a similar technique, starting their writing sessions with letters and journal entries. Time management is key here, though; be sure you ration enough time to complete all your writing tasks.

- **Reread and rewrite what you wrote the day before.** When working on longer documents such as newsletters, proposals, manuals, or reports, reread and edit what you wrote the previous day. As Step 4 explains in even greater detail, this warm-up technique serves several functions: it places you in writing mode; it reminds you of details not contained in your list; and, most important, it allows you to create a better document as you warm up.

Time Management, or the Great Art of Pilfering Minutes

Time management is as central to writing well as flour is to baking bread. Without it, you have words virtually sprinkled across the page, each project an exercise in speed and frustration. But you're far too busy to practice time management. That's the point. *Because* you are so busy, you *must* manage time.

Some businesspeople are experts in the great science of procrastination. Others simply operate on a deadline basis: if the piece is due in five minutes, or if it was due the day before, they start writing it. Imposing time management is relatively simple: just add writing time to your daily calendar. Naturally, you'll need to be flexible. No appointments from 10:00 to 11:00? Plan to write then, knowing the phone will ring and associates will stop by your desk to talk. If your days are particularly splintered with interruptions, throw in an extra hour or so of writing time.

When creating your schedule, be sure to determine the following:

• Which document you should start sooner and which can wait until later in the day. For example, if your employee evaluation should be on the VP's desk by 2:00, better start sometime in the morning. This means saving your less important E-mail message until later that afternoon. Or perhaps you want to jot off that E-mail message as a warm-up and write the more difficult report next.

• A realistic deadline. If that letter should be soaring down the narrow artery of the mail slot by 4:00, start writing it shortly after lunch. Then you can edit your letter later. Have to get information to a client immediately? Plan to write your message, make a quick phone call or take care of some other quick but necessary task, review the message, and fax it.

• Whether you'll need input from others in your organization. If so, leave extra flex time—sometimes hours or even days. This time is especially important when the person providing information or feedback procrastinates or insists you make sweeping changes.

Businesspeople typically fall into their biggest time-management glitches when writing longer documents. Most set aside a few days or, worse, a single day to write that lengthy report or proposal. This means they arrive at the office two hours early when the only one around is the security guard, cancel all appointments, refuse all but the most urgent calls, and type furiously until finally they ship the unedited document via overnight delivery. Then they leave the office, exhausted and arrive home long after everyone else in the Western world has finished dinner. Those who have a home office barricade themselves from family and friends, emerging only for essentials—the bathroom, a sandwich they carry back to their desk, and maybe some fresh air.

Make a Standing Date with Writing

Each morning, look through your schedule book and find the best time to write that day. After two weeks, identify your patterns. For example, some people find regular slices of writing time after lunch when the office is still quiet and they can determine what they need to write. Then, plan to write at that time every day—or every other day—depending on the number of documents you produce.

Now, compare these two scenarios for large projects. In one, the businessperson allocated time, spreading the project over several weeks. In the other, the businessperson used the typical hurry-up-and-write process.

Situation 1
Time: 11:00 A.M., Sunday
Place: Home

Your proposal for a new youth center is due Monday morning. You discussed the contents with your boss two weeks ago. You took notes, reviewed them, and researched additional information at the library. You didn't bother to write during the past week, knowing you had a complete stretch of writing time on Sunday.

So . . . you make a pot of coffee, boot up the computer, and sit at your desk. Okay. You glance at the clock. 11:15. A whole day of writing ahead. You remind yourself: the proposal is due at 9:00 the next morning. You have to write. You must write. You don't have a choice. Maybe if you write well and fast, you'll take a break around 4:00. Maybe make a phone call.

But first you must write. Your upstairs neighbor's phone rings like a sparrow rasping its last. God, you hate distractions. And wouldn't it be nice to go biking? Or maybe take a walk? You can tell from the tips of sunlight darting beneath the curtain that the day is magnificent.

Okay. Buckle down. The report should be at least 20 pages. That's one page every half hour if you write until 9:00 at night. What did you want to say anyway? What if you write too slowly? Or get blocked? You glance at the clock. 11:19. Wow. In only 19 minutes you've become disheartened and pressured. Okay, get a grip, have a sip of coffee. Okay. Begin.

Situation 2
Time: 11:00 A.M., Sunday, two weeks earlier
Place: Home

You learned that you have to write a proposal for a new youth center last Friday. You discussed the contents with your boss and took notes. Sure, you'll have to do a little research in the library, but you might as well start writing early. If you write a little on Sunday, Monday, Wednesday, and Thursday, and research on Tuesday, you should complete the project at least a week early. Then you'll have lead time in case you get stuck or need to do additional research. Good. And, of course, you'll have a chance to rewrite before the proposal is due.

You pour a cup of coffee, boot up the computer, and look at the clock. 11:15. You'll write until 1:00. Then you'll have a little lunch and maybe go for a walk. You can tell from the tips of sun touching the curtains that the day is magnificent. As an incentive, you roll up the curtains. Um, lovely.

The Ultimate, Low-Stress, Fast-and-Effective Writing Diet

Poor writing habits are like a poor diet—they make you sluggish and stressed and cause you to perform well below your potential. The best nourishment for your writing is the following blend.

Create a hospitable writing environment

Not everyone can have a sunny spot overlooking the sea, but try to make your writing environment as clean, quiet, and relaxing as possible. If you work at home, a private room will do. Tack a sign on the door to alert your family that you are writing and are not be to interrupted except in real emergencies—not for sibling spats.

If you are working in an office building, make sure the space around your computer is as clear and relaxing as possible. You may want to have a picture of your family or another favorite photo nearby. Be sure your chair is comfortable and your computer screen set at an appropriate angle.

When possible, write at the same time, in the same place

For many in the business community, where crises flare with every phone call, a consistent writing schedule may be impossible. However, if you have a home office or unusual control over your time, you can build a regular writing time into your day. Most business-people write in the late afternoon when they know how many follow-up letters, informational packets, and other documents they must send out. Or, you may prefer the advantages of early morning: your mind is fresh, thoughts clear, and you're relatively undistracted. Choose what works best for you.

In addition to cutting stress, regular writing times condition your mind to flick into writing mode in the same way that your body grows hungry, sleepy, or tired at the same time every day. They also enable you to complete your writing projects and have greater control over your deadlines.

Don't sit for more than an hour or two at a time

Our bodies are conditioned for many things, but sitting at a computer for long stretches is not one of them. The problems—from bad backs to carpal tunnel syndrome to headaches—have made the headlines of every health magazine in the country. Prolonged sitting also makes you restless, tired, and distracted, which weakens your writing style. The best sitting schedules: one or two hours at a stretch with an hour or two break, or three or four hours with several short breaks in between.

Write in a quiet environment

For most businesspeople—whose offices practically vibrate with ringing phones and conversations—the notion of working in a quiet environment is laughable. But noise is no more generic than the characters in a Western—some are safe and protective, while others are sinister, even deadly.

Safe noise. White noise is as safe as a lullaby. Safer. After all, white noise, including the blur of distant conversations, phones that you *don't* have to answer, and faxes, copiers, and printers, has a harmless, rhythmic beat. White noise blends with the environment into a simple, subtle hush.

Unsafe noise

Conversations. The most common source of unsafe noise is nearby conversation. Whether the conversation centers on the company's new pension plan or a tennis match over the weekend, the moment you start following the trail of discussion, your brain moves away from your writing.

Children. If you work in a home office, children may be another source of unsafe noise. Here's a typical scenario: You're working on an important letter to a prospective client and hear a shrill scream from the living room. You assume your children are just wrestling on the carpet or fighting over a toy. Still, what if one of them fell, cut a finger, banged a head? Even if your spouse or baby-sitter is watching them, you pause and must grope to retrieve those snatches of thought that were heading for the page moments before the interruption.

Music. The most subliminal form of unsafe noise comes from the radio. Surprisingly, people have a flurry of excuses for listening to music when they write, including: "It relaxes me so I can think better," "It puts me in a better mood," and "It creates a nicer environment for writing." The gold medal goes to this line, though: "I don't hear it, so why should I shut it off?" The response: if you don't hear it, why keep it on in the first place?

The truth is, of course, that you *do* hear the music and it *does* affect your writing. When you write, you create a rhythm with your words and sentence structure, which emphasizes important points, enlivens the writing style, and makes the information more appealing for the reader. In a sense, sentence rhythm provides background music for your message. When you listen to the radio, the music deadens your rhythm and causes you to create uniform sentences. The shift between the music and a disc jockeys' announcements also creates distractions that break that valuable flow of thought.

How do you find necessary quiet? If you have a home office, your best course is to plan your writing time around household or street activities. One of my clients lives in an apartment building loaded with college students. As everyone knows, students love music— usually loud music with plenty of bass. At first, my client called his neighbors and reminded them that they shared the building with hard-working elders. The moment that music lowered, though, someone else's music cranked up. Then my client remembered a second well-known fact about students: they love to sleep late. My client's solution was to do his writing in the morning and schedule his meetings at his clients' sites for later in the day. If you have children, you should plan to write when they're at school or day care.

If you work in an unusually noisy office, ask your boss to set up a writing room with a computer and comfortable chair where you and your coworkers can write. Some companies let employees leave work an hour or two early to work on an important proposal or manual in the quiet of home. Other companies are amenable to letting employees come in an hour early when the office is quiet to complete a project, then leave an hour early at the end of the day. If you must stay at your desk, put a Do Not Disturb sign on your cubicle and let voice mail answer the phone.

TRY THIS! Wrestling With Distraction ... and Winning. Create a list of the most common distractions you encounter when writing. Then fold the paper in half lengthwise and write a separate list of solutions. Keep the paper in a desk drawer or folder. Return to it in a week or two. If your solution didn't work, find another.

Problem	*Solution*
Too many phone calls breaking my train of thought.	Use the computer in company library then return to desk to check voice mail every hour or two.
The letters must go out the same afternoon I speak with the client.	Plan to write between 3:00 and 5:00 P.M. and plan to take breaks to return calls, etc.

TRY THIS! Cleaning Home and Office. Look at your writing space and find ways to make improvements. For example, is the space around your computer cluttered with papers? If so, find another place to put them. Is the window closed or dirty? Find ways to let sunlight in for a more relaxing view.

UNDRESSING THIS YEAR'S WRITING FASHIONS

Determining this year's writing fashions is harder than determining what's hot and what's not on the runways. The following undresses today's trends so you can see the naked truth.

Myth 1: Write and Don't Look Back

It's true, some people write their documents without once glancing at the paragraph or line they recently finished. But most people feel tempted to press the Pg Up key on their computers and review that difficult passage, that introductory line, or perhaps that entire page. They look, but are assailed with guilt as voices from their most recent writing workshop rage that they should write and write and write and never digress from the word they recently completed.

Reality: Don't worry, pausing to review portions of your document is more than a guilty pleasure. It helps you follow a train of thought, recapture your writing voice when your energy level wanes or you grow distracted, and gain a sense of achievement.

Myth 2: Writing is Verbal Vomit

Spit out the words, contemporary wisdom says. Don't worry about grammar, person, tense, or even content. Just write and go back later to clean up the mess. This is great news for you, the busy businessperson. So you let the words flow faster than beer on tap. The only trouble—once finished writing, you succumb to the age-old desire to skip rewriting altogether and get the message out, page still messy, inarticulate perhaps, but why should you care? You're on to another task.

Reality: Like runners, writers must find their own pace. Some people can wildly whip through a document and edit later. But most need parameters to give their writing direction. A word doesn't feel right? Find the right one. Tense shifts? Shift it back. Otherwise, you'll be left with an utterly chaotic mess and your editing, if you choose to do it, will take three times longer than necessary.

Myth 3: Good Writers Are Fast Writers

For years clients have told me that they *know* they're terrible writers because they write slowly, as if speed is somehow connected to quality. Never mind that fast writers are often sloppy writers, or that good writers approach each word with consideration even when creating basic instructions.

Reality: Writing fast only works when you write deliberately—diligently following your list of topics, giving yourself breaks when necessary, and leaving editing time before sending out your document.

Myth 4: Don't Take a Break Until You've Completed Your Letter or Memo

You want a cup of tea. Really. The office is cold; your fingers are cold. You ache to feel the warm mug pressed within your palm. Also, you really, *really* need to go to the bathroom; your bladder is pressing within like an overripe melon. Or perhaps you're feeling fidgety and just want to walk across the room and stare mindlessly out the window for a few minutes. But no! You heard from some source somewhere that you should write until your letter is finished. So, miserable, you stay rooted to your seat.

Reality: Getting a little distance from your letter or memo can be healthy and rewarding. Besides, you can't write well when you're uncomfortable—no one can. So, get a cup of tea, make a call, relax a little even though you still have another paragraph or page to go. Ultimately, you'll write faster and your documents will be livelier. Just beware: take necessary breaks; don't create random distractions.

WRITING WELL . . . BUT NOT ALONE

You've probably been there: entangled in the greatest communication trap of all—writing in a group or committee. You most likely walked in willingly, believing that creating that simple letter about the company's new pension plan or establishing a newsletter would be a two- or three-meeting task.

Then, gradually, you became stuck, writing and rewriting and rewriting again as wanted or unwanted feedback seemed to flow from every crack and corner of the company. Suddenly a month had passed and you were *still* working on that letter. Or perhaps two months later that newsletter was still an idea. And you hate to recall the employee manual that took almost a year to complete.

Wait! The next time you embark on a group writing project, follow these time- and energy-saving steps:

1. *Create a three-part plan.* First, give everyone in your group a responsibility, such as gathering information or writing the draft and distributing it for feedback. Next, create a realistic schedule, including time for researching, writing, and rewriting the material. Finally, when appropriate, establish a production budget that will determine the size and style of your document.

2. *Prewrite.* This great time-saver can slash hours or even days of cutting-and-pasting time. Create a list of specific information that belongs in the document. Show this list to decision makers outside the group and adjust it accordingly. If you're creating a document of more than two pages, write a few test paragraphs, gathering consensus about word use and tone *before* tackling huge sections of it. Regardless of your document's size, develop a list of criteria that will create a basis for future feedback. If your company has a style guide, follow it closely.

3. *Write and review the draft.* Once you have written the draft, send copies to other committee members two or three days before the next meeting. This will give everyone a chance to read the material, make comments, and come prepared for a discussion. At the meeting, keep your feedback as objective as possible by being specific. If you think the information sheet you're working on isn't helpful, determine why. Perhaps you don't have enough details. Or perhaps you need a tighter, more chronological structure.

4. *Edit.* Make concrete changes based on the group's feedback. Then, if appropriate, get a round of comments from these sources:

   • Other company representatives, such as the vice president or president, who have a stake in the document.

   • Internal or external customers. Focus groups are great as they allow you to understand the reasoning behind your customers' comments and determine which are relevant and which are not.

   • The legal department, especially when you're writing about procedures, financial matters, or new products or services.

5. *Final edit and design.* Bring the final round of comments to your next meeting. Chances are you can revise right there—tweaking a word, cutting a sentence, adding a slice of information. Then, send your document to the graphic designer—someone on your committee, an in-house employee, or a contractor.

6. *Proof.* Be sure to proofread for those little punctuation problems, grammatical mishaps, and other details that may undermine the professional quality of your work. Remember to proofread on the hard copy, not on the computer. *Warning*: Don't rewrite. Everything on the page has won the group's approval—keep it that way.

Other Top Tips for Group Writing Projects

- Limit the committee to six or seven people. While there's safety in numbers in most situations, large committees only cause confusion.

- Invite decision makers to key meetings such as those at which you're determining content or revising the first draft.

- Invite a professional writer into your group, whether a company technical or marketing writer or an outside consultant. If you're lucky, that person may even write the copy. If not, he or she will provide critical feedback.

- When sending a document for feedback, include the list of criteria you established at the beginning of the process. This will increase the likelihood you'll receive useful and focused feedback.

- Always E-mail or fax material for feedback. Aside from being a time-saver, electronic communication will attract your audience's attention more effectively than either in-house mail or the postal service.

- Edit suggestions into your copy immediately. Waiting even a day or two could have an impact on the effectiveness of your changes.

- Never let the group spend more than a month away from the project or you'll waste time rehashing points.

TROUBLESHOOTING

Everyone occasionally has problems writing. Sometimes the problems vanish with as little fanfare as they appeared; sometimes they stick around for weeks or even months; and sometimes they make a grand entrance and move in for good. Ideally, writing problems should be like those annoying relatives who visit once every third decade for a day or two—just find the right one-way ticket and they're out of your life. Here are a few ways to overcome the most common writing problems.

Rx for Writer's Block

Just because you dislike writing—or find certain subjects about as appetizing as last week's pizza—doesn't mean you're blocked. But if you suspect a block has infiltrated your system, check for these symptoms:

- Trouble finishing a document
- Inability to write certain documents
- Inability to write at all
- Anxiety that frequently grows debilitating
- Serious to deadening reaction to writing under pressure

Think of a block as a muscle cramp; loosen up and the problem will pass. Your exercises may vary from the warm-ups you read about in the first part of this chapter to the exercises that follow. But, like an athlete, you must practice these exercises deliberately and consistently for the best results. Now, try these:

1. This is the no-fuss method of breaking blocks. Just write for two minutes every morning—no more and no less. Don't worry about word use, spelling, grammar, or even content. If you're writing by hand, ignore penmanship. Cross out freely. Stuck? Write about being stuck. Be sure to speed write each morning at the same time for at least a week or two. That way you'll set your internal clock for writing mode.

2. Find a partner—spouse, friend, or coworker—who will pick an object for you to write about before work each day. The objects may be basic, such as an apple or a flag, or more complex, such as your favorite vacation spot or your childhood house. You need to write only one paragraph, but feel free to write more if you like. Then show your writing to your partner. Have that person tell you what he or she *likes* about your writing. If you're inspired, move on to more complex ideas, such as describing your most frightening experience or your strongest childhood memory.

3. Write a letter every other day for two weeks straight, even on weekends. Make sure you're writing to someone you trust. Don't know what to say? Explain why you're writing. Afraid your style is stiff? Uncomfortable? Throw the document away, but only after you've finished. Otherwise, send the letter. In the process you'll build positive associations with writing and feel more in control.

4. Write about some aspect of work—your boss, your employees, your customers, or the barrage of responsibilities you confront each time you walk in the door. Don't worry if you make sense, just get the words out. If you're writing by hand, throw the paper away. If you're on the computer, print the piece, then throw it away. In the process, you'll loosen up, put your writing in context, and gain a stronger sense of control.

On Your Mark, Get Set, GO! (Really!)

Is this your problem? You're ready to write, a cup of steaming coffee beside your desk, your computer booted up, the office unusually quiet; best yet, you know exactly what to say, only . . . you just . . . can't . . . seem . . . to get . . . started. If so, join the thousands and thousands of businesspeople who claim that opening paragraphs are like cement blocks on their writing feet.

The solution is remarkably simple. Ignore the opening and jump into the body of your message. When you finish, go back and add that delinquent first paragraph or mold the first line of your body into an eloquent opening. Perhaps, though, you approach writing as a builder approaches a house. Without that first layer of bricks, the whole thing topples. If you *must* have an opening paragraph, then do this: write two or three alternatives. Write quickly, too, knowing that you're merely creating options, however strong or weak they turn out.

The Ants-in-the-Pants Syndrome

When you were younger, you called it ants in the pants. As an adult, you call it distraction. Whatever you call it, the inability to sit still for more than a few moments plagues many businesspeople—particularly those who prefer undergoing minor surgery to writing. The moment you decide you *must* make a cup of tea or absolutely *must* make that phone call, stop and set a goal. Tell yourself that you'll take a break after you finish two more paragraphs. Or decide that you'll write until half past the hour. That way, you'll have the naughty pleasure of the distraction *and* accomplish your task.

Remember, don't force yourself to sit for too long. This is harmful to both your body and your mind.

CONCLUSION

Smooth, swift writing can be blocked by old ghosts, distracting environments, or lack of practice. But now you know how to break through these barriers and let in the spontaneity critical to exciting word use.

Rewriting for Structure

Object: *To eliminate structural problems without having to reread your document or waste time cutting and pasting paragraphs.*

The Triple-Benefit Rewriting Process

Ernest Hemingway once said: "There's no such thing as writing—only rewriting." In the business world this translates into: "The best way to communicate isn't through writing—only rewriting." Yet, once most businesspeople finish the writing stage and are ready to rewrite, they make one of these mistakes:

1. In spite of their best intentions, they end up shuffling words around the page rather than actually making improvements.

2. They think rewriting is too time-consuming and send the document out the moment that last period hits the page.

With a minimal amount of solid rewriting, you can reap some surprising benefits. Most obviously, you'll end up with a stronger document, one that reaches your readers immediately and glides them from one point to the next. The second benefit is long lasting; in fact, it lasts a lifetime. By rewriting quickly and conscientiously, you'll actually improve your writing skill in a matter of weeks. Finally, as your writing style improves, you'll need to rewrite less and can triple your writing tempo. Sound like one of those too-good-to-be-true ads, like "Lose 50 pounds in one week"? Actually, *Words at Work*'s unique rewriting method is based on logical principles that require practice and commitment. Here's what you do.

1. Once you finish writing, put your document aside

Where do I get the time for this? you're wondering. If you followed the time-management principles presented in step 2 you've already reserved a pocket of editing time. Often, though, you'll have to create documents unexpectedly thanks to a phone call from a VP, a demanding customer, or a potential customer who needs your company's information by 5:01—and no later—that day. In these cases, write your document immediately. Then let it sit while you write a new document, make phone calls, or get that cup of coffee you've been promising yourself.

How long should your document sit? Three minutes is good—ten minutes is better. Three hours is even better than that. But don't let your document wait several days or longer. While absence makes the heart grow fonder in romance novels, it makes the memory dim in the business world and may distance you from your message.

2. Locate specific problems

No question about it, rewriting can waste time. You may recall long afternoons combing through an especially important document, trying to catch problems as elusive as trout in a spring-fed pond. Rather than create stronger copy, you probably shuffled the words around, unsure of what changes you were making and why. Most likely, only one or two bad habits permeate your writing. Clean them up, and your writing will improve significantly.

The problem, of course, is that most people are not aware of their bad habits. Think, for example, of the times close friends or relatives have pointed out that you were chewing with your mouth open or driving embarrassingly slowly in the fast lane of the highway, a small caravan behind you. You were probably surprised and stopped yourself the next time your fork left your mouth or your foot rested on the gas pedal too lightly.

The Secret Passion
(or, How Rewriting Saved My Client's Writing Dreams)

Many years ago, I had a client—a management consultant—with a great passion for everything she did. Each week, she'd appear at my office impeccably dressed, nails perfectly manicured, hair teased into a perfect flip. For an hour, we'd discuss her ideas for articles on everything from manager-employee relationships to productive ways companies could see their employees through mergers.

Perhaps my client's greatest passion was her writing. She didn't want to write well—she wanted to write perfectly. She didn't want to publish in a local paper—she wanted her articles picked up by major papers everywhere. We reviewed the finer points of article writing, from an interesting lead, to fact-filled quotes, to a strong and compelling angle. We combed through her work separating weak words from strong ones, turning over her content for meaning.

Then, at last, she wrote an article. She dropped it on my desk, face flushed, meticulous hairdo slightly rustled. "This better be good!" she proclaimed. "I rewrote it five times."

I read the article. I wished I could rush to the phone and alert every editor to this marvelous piece of writing. I couldn't. During those five rewrites, my client had busily shuffled her mistakes on the paper, attempting in some vague, even abstract way to make her document better. Her biggest mistake—repeated words and ideas—still cluttered the document, distorting her message as a fun-house mirror distorts a reflection. Somewhat defeated, she went home.

The story has a happy ending, however. This driven woman spent the next week conscientiously identifying, then correcting, those troublesome repeats. Not long after, her dream came true. A large city newspaper published her well-written—and rewritten—article, and several others picked it up soon after.

Writing is the same. Chances are you don't realize you write in the passive voice, you're wordy, or you use boring sentence structure. So, how do you identify your bad habits? Use the exercises that follow and then, as discussed in step 5, ask someone for objective feedback.

> **CAUTION!**
>
> Once you're aware of your bad habits, don't try to monitor them *as* you write. This will only slow down your writing process and may create blocks. Or, equally bad, you'll feel frustrated and regress to your old style. Instead, write as you normally would, and check for bad habits later.

3. Correct the problem

Correcting your writing problems might sound daunting at worst, annoying at best. It shouldn't. Rewriting is much like working on a puzzle. Shift the pieces around, take out a piece, add a piece, and you've got it: a complete picture of what you want to say! As you'll see, rewriting, like all aspects of the writing process, requires a few strategic, and predictable, moves, with as little guesswork as possible.

And here's the real beauty of this stage of writing: by working on one bad habit consistently for several weeks, you ultimately break that habit. Most likely you won't even be aware that you're breaking it. Suddenly you'll notice your documents need less rewriting, which, of course, means you're creating a better document . . . faster! And, though you should always rewrite, and your writing can always improve, the writing process will grow less painful, even enjoyable.

Growing A Message

I once had an editor who described the function of rewriting wonderfully. He said writing was like a growing tree. Spontaneity allows little branches to shoot out, making the message lush and beautiful. But for the writing to be healthy, you need to prune it back, give it shape, cutting back one idea, propping up another.

STOP!

Before you continue with this chapter, determine which mode of rewriting suits your style.

The one-habit-at-a-time mode

Sure, you confront several writing problems each time you rewrite a new document. Most people do. But that lone bad habit burns through your writing like a blowtorch, outshining all the others. One of my clients—a professional writer at an insurance company—was like this. This writer was mature, serious about her work, and willing to improve. Too willing, in fact. Her problems: tired expressions and general rather than specific words. More significant, she used ten words where two would do, creating dull, unwieldy documents.

In her zeal to improve her writing, she tried correcting all three problems each time she wrote. The result: she spent an absurd amount of time rewriting, didn't rewrite especially well, and eventually grew so frustrated she stopped rewriting altogether. This, of course, concerned her manager. After all, she was receiving a clean $80,000 salary to produce flimsily written copy. At that point I recommended that she revise for one bad habit at a time, starting with the master bad habit, wordiness.

The benefits of this approach were threefold. First, since wordiness accounted for 75 percent of the problem, my client improved each document significantly. Second, by focusing exclusively on wordiness, she overcame the habit sooner. Third, her wordiness had overwhelmed the other problems, making them more difficult to identify; once she cut words, the rest of her writing became more manageable.

The equal-time-to-equal-habits mode

You have several different but equal bad habits. Say, for example, your points spread all across the page, ruining your structure. In addition, your tone is negative—even the most friendly letter sounds like a threat. Both problems interfere with your communication equally and predictably.

In this case, your best weapon is two-pronged. First, rewrite for structure. Then, attack negative tone. Don't spend too long rewriting for either problem; give an equal amount of time to both. Of course, sometimes you may have only a minute or two to rewrite, your reader literally standing by a fax in some office 2,000 miles away. In this case, quickly rewrite for the most glaring problem. If you're offering a solution to a problem your organization caused, rewrite for the positive voice. If you're sending difficult instructions to a reader with a .01 second attention span, focus on structure.

The chain-reaction mode

Just about everyone faces a situation in which one writing problem creates another. The best rewriting method in this case is the simplest: by correcting one problem you chip away at the others. Again, take wordiness. Many wordy business writers also use tired expressions. Ax away extra words, and you also enliven your writing. You should still spot-check for humdrum words and phrases. But you will find only an eighth of the original number.

TRY THIS! Take out a piece of paper and several writing samples from the portfolio you collected when starting this book. Then read through the following section on introductions. Compare your writing to the samples here and be proactive! Note any weaknesses, so you can catch them in your next document.

CATCH-AND-KEEP-THEM OPENINGS

The best place to start rewriting is with your first paragraph, where you should assert your point and immediately engage your readers. Next, rework the body of your document before touching other words. Here's why: when making structural changes, you'll probably

> ## IMAGINE THIS
>
> Imagine that your document is a cliff that your readers are scaling. You must lead them carefully, strategically, step by excruciating step or they will lose their footing and fall. The toeholds are your transitions, taking them from one thought to the next; the substance of your message is the solid surface, keeping them from sliding on loose particles; the benefit of reading your document is the view that waits ahead.

need to shift, cut, and break paragraphs into sections, tossing words around like dice at a crapshoot. If you rewrite for word use first, you might waste time refining words you'll eventually cut. In addition, you'll probably need to backtrack, revisiting transitions and other words and phrases you already covered.

What's Your Opening Line?

Four seconds is too long. Three seconds is too long. When writing, you must snag your readers' attention in the time they take to click a TV remote—approximately one second, or, in writing terms, four words. Just as important, you must compete with the volumes of sales and marketing materials that reach their homes and offices daily, some of it as tasteless as Elvis on velvet.

A good illustration is a piece I received in the mail yesterday. On the cover, a sketch of the infamous Dick Clark and Ed McMahon. Just above the picture, a message that looked like this:

If you have & return winning prize claim number, we'll say . . .

SUSAN BENJAMIN, YOU'VE CLEARED THAT FINAL HURDLE— YOU'RE MASSACHUSETTS' TOP WINNER—GUARANTEED A FULL $11,000,000!

Naturally, my attention immediately went to the $11 million line, my heart doing a thump and a half at my sudden luck. I didn't even notice that qualifying comment—about how I had to have that elusive winning claim number—until I searched for it. Just beneath was another shamelessly misleading notice:

URGENT WARNING:

Enclosed documents are extremely sensitive.
$2,000.00 FINE OR 5 YEARS IMPRISONMENT
or both for any person who tampers with or obstructs delivery of mail
intended for someone else: U.S. Code Title 18, Sec. 1702

What a setup! This urgent notice applies to any mailed document, from your child's note from summer camp to a parking ticket. Yet some clever PR team positioned it so that it appears to apply to the sweepstakes letter only. So, how do you compete, while maintaining a business tone *and* professional integrity? You can't give away $11 million. But you can personalize your message by following these tips.

Discard those has-been openings. Sure, they're as comforting as an old sweater, but how many times have you read or written this:

> I enjoyed speaking with you on the phone last week.

This line is so overdone it sounds completely insincere. The alternative lies in unique and specific words. And no, you don't have to be a Pulitzer Prize winner to use them. Nor must you spend hours oozing a heartfelt message. Instead, be exact. You enjoyed speaking to your reader? What did you enjoy talking about? If you talked about some changes in your reader's company you might write:

> Thanks for sharing your insights into TeleCom's plans.

If you're writing a sales document, you may have had a long and friendly conversation with your potential customer. Start with an "I hope . . ." opening that recalls the personal side of your conversation. For example, if your client mentioned that he or she was taking two weeks off to go hiking in the mountains, you could start the letter with this line:

> I hope you had a great two weeks away—the weather certainly was perfect for hiking.

Or perhaps you acted on information your reader passed along during your conversation. Then you'd write:

> I immediately contacted John Houghton after we talked on Friday.

This is especially significant when you're answering complaints:

> Thank you for letting me know about the error with your bill. Since we spoke, I have met with our accounting vice president, who supplied the necessary information.

Now, consider this proposal line:

> Our company is committed to meeting your needs.

Frankly, no one cares about your company's commitment. Rather, readers care about your company's action and how it will affect them. Are you having a 40-percent-off sale? Tell them that. Avoid little words and phrases that bore even the most intrigued audience, such as "As you probably know." If your readers probably know it, why say it? Cut the phrase. Look at this line:

> I wanted to write you to tell you about our special 40% off by-invitation-only sale.

Again, a bore. The opening is so dense the reader probably won't hack to the end where the really important message lies waiting. Cut and flip the words so you have:

> Please attend our special, by-invitation-only 40% off sale.

Or, you could emphasize the "by invitation only" and "40% off" points by placing them first in the sentence:

> Please attend our by-invitation-only, 40% off sale on November 9.

Look at this deadweight from an all-too-typical business letter:

> Enclosed please find the data you requested.

The revision could be more personal:

> As I promised on Monday, I'm sending along data about Pilgrim National's retirement plans.

Or, you could embed the "enclosed," in something interesting about the enclosure:

> As the enclosed data reveal, 65% of all Californians prefer our plans over all others.

The All-Time Most Tired Letter Openings

1. Enclosed please find ...
2. Pursuant to our conversation ...
3. Per your request ...
4. Enclosed herewith ...
5. Thank you for speaking with me on the phone ...
6. We'd like to introduce you to ...
7. I enjoyed speaking with you ...
8. I am writing you this letter to ...
9. This letter will ...
10. I want to introduce myself ...
11. My company's mission is to ...
12. At my company, we are committed to ...
13. At my company, we believe ...
14. Did you know that ...
15. Do you want to ...

TRY THIS! Look through your portfolio for tired opening lines. Then write two or three interesting alternatives for each. The next time you write, use those instead.

Create a strong reader focus. Target what the reader will get from your message, rather than what you'll give. Say you wrote this line for a brochure:

> At Millboro Industries, we believe that quality is critical to our customers. That is why our engineers inspect all our products twice before delivery.

The message focuses entirely on Millboro Industries. Shift the words a little, and you have:

> Since quality is critical to your success, our engineers inspect all our products twice before delivering them.

In other cases you might write a line like this one:

> We wanted to let you know that we are giving a tote bag and a CD of Beethoven's 9th Symphony with every $50 donation you make to our station.

Here is a classic example of missed opportunity. Rather then tell your readers immediately about the free gift, this line focuses unnecessarily on the radio station, placing "we" twice in the first eight words. Instead, write:

> You'll receive a tote bag and a CD of Beethoven's 9th Symphony with every $50 donation you make to our station.

Use lively, interesting devices. The following devices are great openings for sales letters, brochures, annual reports, and many other types

Writer focus	*Reader focus*
We wanted to let you know about recent changes in the building's management.	Please know that your building has new managers.
The sales seminar will cover three important tools for contacting a customer.	In this seminar you'll gain three important tools for successfully contacting customers.
We train our employees to be customer relations representatives so you have the best possible service.	So you have the best possible service, we train all our employees to be customer representatives.
To show our appreciation to you, our employees, we're hosting a special, summer fiesta picnic.	Come to a special summer fiesta picnic in your honor.
We are sending you a newsletter with an update on the city's tax changes.	For an update on the city's tax read the enclosed newsletter.

of documents. At first, you may need to spend time mulling over which is right for your message or audience, but soon you'll know instinctively.

1. Anecdotes. People love stories, whether they're about the stock market or the latest trends in health care. That's why short anecdotes—one or two paragraphs—open documents so nicely. The stories should be true and intriguing and have a smooth chronological order that moves readers from point to point. Here's a good example from a brochure about a small grocery store that evolved into a national supermarket chain:

> It was 1905. It was the year Ben Hersowitz and his wife, Hannah, opened a small grocery store in New York City. It was also the year immigrants arrived from all over Europe.

> In their new and often difficult environment, Ben and
> Hannah's new neighbors struggled for basic provisions—
> milk, flour, eggs. The Hersowitzes knew they needed to
> help, and established a special credit system and a work-for-
> food exchange to keep their young neighborhood strong.
>
> It was in the spirit of community involvement and high-
> quality products that Ben and Hannah's store grew over
> the next century to become SuperMart, one of the world's
> largest supermarket chains. Of course, a lot has changed
> since 1905, and we've added radios, televisions, lawn
> furniture, and even pets to our shelves.

To find the right anecdotes, stay alert when you're in the office, reading the paper, and talking with coworkers. If you find an interesting piece, but don't think you'll use it soon, clip it anyway. You may have an opportunity to use it later.

2. Descriptions. You'd be amazed at the versatility of a descriptive lead. Obviously they're great for introducing concrete items—people, buildings, even food. But you can also use descriptions for ideas or services.

Why are descriptions so effective? For many reasons. First, descriptions force you to use specific words, making the message more revealing and interesting. When describing a property, for example, you need to say more than "It's big." You need to show *how* big—3 acres or 44.

Second, descriptions help your readers take in your message more completely. Instead of simply reading it, they may see it, smell it, hear it, and even feel it, depending on the information you provide. The result: your readers have a whole experience, will be more interested, and will remember your message longer.

When creating descriptions, remember that structure is key. Don't jump from point to point, but move the reader from one characteristic to the next in a flowing order, using appropriate transitions. Here's an example:

> You can't see it—but every time you pick up the phone it's
> there. It's strong, too—strong enough to bring you across the
> world in moments. And it's there when you want it to be—
> whether you're in your car, at home, or at the office. It's our
> new telephone service. It's cheaper that MCI, Sprint, or AT&T.
> It can be yours with a phone call.

3. Quotes. When professionals think of quotes, they usually think of JFK, Winston Churchill, Abe Lincoln, and other high-profile, usually deceased, sources. Numerous writers have books laden with quotes for every occasion alongside their dictionaries and style guides. But you can quote anyone, from a young child who says something innocent yet insightful, to a journalist whose article supports your case.

Quotes sound different from the narrative voice. This contrast gives your writing the texture and color it needs to fully intrigue your readers—from the first line to the last of your introductory paragraph. Quotes also accentuate your point. For example, quoting a manager on the inside scoop at a software company is more convincing than simply summarizing his or her perspective. Finally, quotes, simply by being embraced by quotation marks or set in italics, will attract your readers. The next trick, of course, is following the quote with an equally intriguing and inviting line of your own. Look at this example from a wine seller's brochure:

> **"Good living is the best revenge."—Oscar Wilde**
> You and your employees had a hard week. You worked
> overtime to finish a project with a drop-dead deadline. Your
> competition is edging in on your best client. And the cash flow
> has become a drip and clog. It's the end of the week and you
> want . . . revenge. How? By opening a bottle of Vineyard's best
> wine and letting the good living begin.

4. Dialogue. Dialogue also gives readers an interesting-sounding, firsthand account of information directly linked to your subject. And since dialogue occurs between two or more parties, readers get the feeling they're eavesdropping on some spicy conversation. The better the dialogue, the more intriguing or suggestive the content, the more your readers will want to keep reading.

Your problem is finding this dialogue. Quote books exist, but dialogue books don't. Newspapers and magazines are great sources if you remember to keep alert while reading and record usable portions as you go. You can always use hypothetical situations. But beware of creating stiff, unlikely language or boring expressions. Keep the language as compelling and fresh as possible, drawing your reader into the body of your piece:

> Does this scene seem familiar?
>
> *Father:* A counselor from your school called today and told me a lot of students have been taking drugs. She wanted me to talk to you about it.
>
> *Son:* Don't bother me, Dad.
>
> *Father:* This is important. Drugs can kill, you know.
>
> *Son:* Just leave me alone, Dad. You don't know anything about it.
>
> If you want help getting your son or daughter to open up about drugs call the National Center for Drug Education. We'll provide you with brochures, information sheets, even films to help you talk with your children. You can bet your child's life on it.

5. True-or-false statements. True-or-false statements are document openers. They create tension and actively engage readers in your message. They also have a unique, gamelike quality, daring readers to guess the right answer. And they establish a friendly yet professional tone, using interesting, staccato sentence rhythms.

Your biggest task is to make your true or false statements challenging for your readers. Perhaps you want to undermine old notions. Or give a new slant to commonly known facts. Regardless of your objective, you must provide startling, lesser-known information that immediately connects to your message. Look at this opening from a health insurance company's brochure:

> *True or false?* Only 10% of college students eventually find careers in their majors.
>
> *True.* Most lose interest once they enter the real world and find work in other areas.

6. Facts. Objective information—especially statistics, percentages, and dollar amounts—is a great opener. For starters, it's reliable, giving readers concrete information that will intrigue, interest, and, perhaps, astonish them. In addition, it gives credibility to your message while underscoring your point.

Mentioning a specific source, whether the *Wall Street Journal* or a government report, can enhance the validity of your facts. Sometimes, however, you may want to keep your source more general, particularly when your company initiated the study you're quoting. For example, rather than say:

> We recently conducted a study that showed dogs who eat our Protein Plus dog food live up to two years longer than other dogs of the same breed.

write:

> One recent study showed that dogs who eat Yam's Protein Plus dog food live up to two years longer than other dogs of the same breed.

Beware of common facts. Use only vibrant and surprising information.

7. Specific advantages. Sad, but true: in business writing, anyway, readers care more about themselves than about you. That's why mentioning specific advantages at the beginning is a surefire way to lure your readers into a brochure, proposal, direct mail piece, or any other type of document. The trick here, as with other openings, is to stay *reader focused*. Look at this example:

> You get more than one month's free checks at Commerce Bank and Trust. You get a special information center, ready to advise you about the best investments, the most suitable loans, and the highest-interest savings account for you. And you get something no other bank provides: an advisory center with information on which stockbrokers, accountants, and independent bookkeepers are the best—and most trustworthy—in the state.

8. Contrasting points. Showing the differences and, possibly, the similarities between two services or ideas can be a great way to play up the ultimate advantages of one of them. Just be sure that the advantages are quantifiable and will truly interest your readers. In this example, the writer provides the reader with money-saving tips for purchasing generic products in the wholesale center:

> What's the difference between 4.5 pounds of the leading laundry detergent and our leading no-brand variety? About $2.00.

9. Problems and solutions. This is a great setup for almost any type of document, provided you have provocative, complex problems and sensible solutions. Here, you can promise results to one organization by showing how you brought them to another. Or, you can use the problem-solution setup to convince your readers to take an action by showing the results that action brought others. In addition, problem-solution setups have an engaging, anecdotal quality. Take this example from a direct mail piece:

> Tom Sutherland of Norwood Corporation had a problem. He had to design and copy information sheets and

brochures introducing his company's new product for an
important trade show . . . in two days. This already difficult
task was even more difficult since two of his employees
were out sick and the other three were working on
important assignments. And, Tom was working on a tight
budget. That's when Tom called us.

10. Questions. Questions are the most used introductory
option. They are also the most abused. They tend to lie flat, stagnant
on the page, asking readers to respond to such obvious inquiries as
these:

Are you interested in saving money?

Tired of paying too much on your heating bills?

The readers' response: a big sigh and a rustle as they turn the page.
Yet questions really *are* a great device. They sound interesting, make
a refreshing change from the usual period-ending statement, and
create tension, compelling the reader to continue to the answer—
and beyond.

To create absorbing questions, remember to follow these three
simple rules:

a. *Answer the question immediately.* Frequently, business writers
ask questions and neglect to answer them, opting instead to
provide related, yet loosely connected information. This dis-
turbs the structure, distracts the reader, and makes the question irrelevant. If you want to withhold an answer for a few
paragraphs, fine, but make sure your readers know one is
coming soon.

b. *Provide information as you ask.* You have absolutely no room
for fluff anywhere in your document—especially in the opening. That's why every word of your question must give your
readers concrete information. The best way to achieve this is

through specifics. Look at this opening from a newsletter article for home owners:

> Thirty-five percent of local houses will be robbed this year; will yours be one of them? Where does your house rank in a recent government test for safety and security?

c. *Use interesting language.* Make sure your question sounds sincere by avoiding clichéd and tired expressions and keeping your wording lively and specific.

TRY THIS! Rewrite these openings using different devices:

1. Did you know that our employees use over a ton of paper a year? And that much of that paper goes into the wastebasket to become just so much more environmental waste? Did you also know that the white cardboard boxes outside the elevators on every floor will recycle that paper and in the process, minimize pollution?

2. Everyone said Molly Slater was pretty. She had enviable red hair, pale green eyes, and skin pale as milkweed. Molly knew how to dress, too, always wearing tailored suits, with perfectly coordinated accessories, from her pinkie ring to her buttons. Molly had only one problem: she weighed 380 pounds.

TRY THIS! Rewrite the beginnings of several of your most recent documents in two or three ways. With response letters, determine ways to connect with the reader. Be sure to keep the first four words of your opening line especially strong.

Moving Along: The Rest of Your First Paragraph

Another must for your first paragraph is an action statement in the third or fourth line that gives your readers the nugget of your information. Then, even if they only skim the rest of your document or read a line or two of the body and throw the rest away, you'll up your chances of eliciting the response you want. Look at this example:

> Thank you for contacting us about the difficulty you had collecting your baggage at the Oakland airport. We are very sorry for the inconvenience this has caused you. As you know, traveling can create problems of this sort regardless of how careful the airline personnel might be.
>
> To receive compensation, please send us a detailed list of the items that you lost and complete the gray areas of the enclosed form.

Although apologizing for the organization's mistakes is essential, customers want results. By the second paragraph, the reader is already frustrated and may even have picked up the phone to call the customer relations department. Or, the reader may have merely skimmed the second paragraph and sent back an incomplete form. By relocating information, the company is more likely to get the results it wants:

> We are very sorry for the inconvenience you experienced regarding your lost luggage. So that you can receive compensation as quickly as possible, please send us a detailed list of the items that you lost and complete the gray areas of the enclosed form.

Sometimes you simply want to give your readers important information. Again, get that important information into the second or third line of your introductory paragraph:

> Thank you for contacting us with your concerns about our recent merger with Kell Company. Please be assured, we are

> combining forces and do not intend to lay off any of the customer representatives you know and trust. In addition, we will keep the branch on Holmes Street open for the usual hours.

In other cases, the point of your opening, particularly for an instructional piece or proposal, is to entice your readers to keep reading. Give them an immediate reason:

> As you will see in the following proposal, Thomson and Hart can save you up to $500,000 a year while providing significantly better service than what you currently receive.

When writing instructions, mention advantages first, actions second. This gives your readers a reason for taking the appropriate steps—completely and in the order you provided:

> Congratulations on purchasing the Bouncy Bouncer—a fun way for infants from four to fourteen months to build their muscles while improving their coordination. To quickly and easily assemble your Bouncy Bouncer, please follow these instructions carefully.

Finally—Don't stumble on these unsettling openings

Make sure you don't stumble over otherwise smooth openings by falling into these tired traps.

Oldies but not goodies. Sometimes you need to write about an event—an important meeting, a precedent-setting legal decision, or a new product announcement—that occurred several weeks ago. Several weeks isn't long . . . in a person's lifetime. But it's eons in the business world. That's why you should never begin a newsletter article, brochure, sales letter, or almost any other document with a date that's more than one day old. Look at this example from a memo to employees at a computer software company that was dated September 15:

> On September 10, President Ron Foreman announced that he would be resigning after a decade with the company. He made this announcement at the Board of Trustees' annual retreat.

The opening—September 10—is hardly interesting. This alternative is certainly an improvement:

> President Ron Foreman will resign after a decade with the company. He announced his decision at the annual Board of Trustees' retreat on September 10.

If you're telling the reader about today's event or a procedure that will begin immediately, start with the date. This is especially important for memos, call-for-action letters, press releases, and newsletter articles for weekly publications. Here are examples from a press release and a memo:

> Today, Mission, Inc., announced that it has launched the third in its series of software products.

> On June 14, the company will move to the Walnut Building.

Old dates are boring, but really old dates—from 25 to 250 years old—become interesting again. For example, notice how the date intrigues the reader in this paragraph from a citizen committee's action letter:

> In 1930, Subsquant County was in trouble. The depression had just become a reality and the citizens were scared. In 1997, Subsquant County is in trouble again. The city council wants to implement new tax laws that will throw our county back to the bleak economic climate of 60 years past.

No-name openings. Everyone loves gossip. The newspaper and television news is loaded with *who*s rather than *what*s, telling us more about military leaders than the causes they fight for, more about the personalities in the Senate than the policies they expound. For this reason, try to start your document with a *who*, such as the company president, a controversial or much-loved local political figure, or a celebrity:

> Colin Powell will deliver the keynote address.

But beware of starting your piece with an unknown's name. For example, if you're writing an announcement for a special training session, don't say:

> Dr. Gilbert Milton, psychologist and stress specialist, will speak about stress-relieving techniques this Friday in Conference Room B.

After all, why should your readers care about some stranger? On the other hand, his position is interesting. Look at the difference in this line:

> Psychologist and stress specialist Dr. Gilbert Milton will speak about stress-relieving techniques this Friday in Conference Room B from 1:00 to 2:00.

Of course, you could jazz up your message in these ways:

> Stressed? Then relax and learn how to stay relaxed with psychologist and stress specialist Dr. Gilbert Milton this Friday in Conference Room B from 1:00 to 2:00.

> If you want to relax in Bermuda but don't have a plane ticket, do the next best thing and attend psychologist and stress specialist Dr. Gilbert Milton's seminar on stress-relieving techniques this Friday in Conference Room B from 1:00 to 2:00.

CREATING AN APPEALING BODY

Revising the structure of your document can be akin to piecing together bits of shattered glass. The longer the document, the more complicated the message, the more difficult—and essential—the task. Why? Think about your normal revision process. You look at the page, notice a comma's out of place, one period too many lies at the end of your sentence, the beginning of your letter is cliché. You're relying on visual tip-offs to guide you from one problem to the next. But those are little things. The body of your document can encompass from 1 to 300 pages or more. You're trapped by sheer physical reality—you cannot possibly see whether your points move quickly and evenly.

The trap grows even more complex once you try to revise. Where should you put that ill-fitting but essential point? When you've repeated a point one, two, or three times, where should you cut? And when should you repeat a message? And, perhaps the most important question, How do you escape, Houdini-like, from the chains of words?

The answer—the first step in this book—is to create a list *before* writing. That way, you'll significantly increase the odds that your points will flow evenly and you'll have fewer structural changes to make. A list does something more, though. It helps you see your points in one self-contained area. Simply make sure that each point on your list has a parallel point in your document. Find a problem? Change it, using your list to guide you.

Check transitions

Transitions are red flags signaling whether your piece flows or wanders. For short, complicated documents, such as letters giving complex instructions, check the transitions in every paragraph. They should take you clearly from one action to the next.

For longer documents, you'll have two sets of transitions. One set connects the thoughts in your paragraphs. The other connects larger portions of your document. Again, make sure that your transitions flow. For example, if you start with "one," as in one reason, one point, or one fact, make sure that "two" and "three" follow. If you mention that an event began at 8:00 A.M., you'd better tell the reader what happened at 10:00 and 12:00.

However, don't jump back in time without giving your readers clear signposts, as in this example:

> Joan Garth announced the changes at 2:00 today. She warned us about their scope last week.

What do askew transitions tell you? Two possibilities. The first, more optimistic message is that your points are fine—don't worry—but your transitions are problematic. So backtrack, adjust or add them, and keep going. When you write your next document, make sure the transitions are solidly placed.

The second possibility is the more likely one. Missing transitions mean holes riddle your structure. You need to shuffle here and there, making sure your order is as sensible as good walking shoes. Perhaps you should determine your structure again, this time using transitions more conscientiously. Perhaps you should tweak that line or paragraph that throws the structure off. Be sure to make adjustments. Otherwise, you can promise yourself one thing: your readers will make the first paragraph of your document the last.

Create an outline

The outline. Yes, the one you remember so fondly from high school. Use this outline only *after* you've written long or complex pieces. It will tell you where you've traveled, like a scrapbook without pictures. Just return to the beginning of your document and chart each point, each bit of support, each reference as you go. Use the most comfortable structure, too—those numerals and letters. Have you repeated a point, omitted information, or veered from your original list? Restructure on your outline, then revise the document itself.

Look at this section of an outline for a newsletter article about vacationing at bed and breakfasts.

I. Dogs
  A. What to consider when deciding whether to bring one
    I. Trouble finding the right bed and breakfasts

    2. Whether dog will fight with other dogs or cats
      who reside at B&B
  B. The dos and don'ts of pet etiquette
    1. DO
      a. ask for the best place to walk your dog
      b. feed dog in parking lot or away from B&B
    2. DO NOT
      a. bring dog to breakfast table
      b. allow dog to bark, yip, or trot around
      c. leave dog hairs in your room after your visit
II. Location
  A. What to consider when deciding on a location
    1. proximity to sights
    2. proximity to public transportation
    3. amount of parking
  B. Compare country and city settings
    1. noise
    2. safety
    3. hours guests can come and go

Look for repeated words

A sure tip-off that you have structural problems is repeated ideas. The most obvious clue: repeated words that rest on the page like ash after a fire. Simply isolate the culprit, cut, and smooth out the surrounding transitions. Since you might naturally repeat a word as you discuss one person or idea, be careful to preserve valuable information.

Of course, your word use may vary, and finding repeated ideas may be like trying to find a stranger at a Halloween party. Your best recourse, outside of returning to your list or outlining anew, is to mark each paragraph or section with signs, such as stars or circles, representing the points they include. Then, compare the sections to ensure that you're presenting fresh information or mentioning new facts about old topics.

ENDINGS THAT SIGH OR SING

Why must closing paragraphs be as strong as opening ones? Though closing paragraphs are the last ones your readers will see, they're the first they'll remember. Besides, your readers' behavior is as unpredictable as their eating habits or love lives. Many read the first paragraph, skim the body, and read the closing. Others read only the beginning and closing paragraphs. Don't risk weakening your message with a sickly closing.

The information that belongs in your last paragraph depends on the type of document you're writing. Look at the following table for a few pointers:

Document	Closing	Example
Memos	Finish your message. No special closings necessary. If appropriate, mention future plans.	If you need more materials, please contact Donna at ext. 213.
Letters	Mention future plans and enclosures unless they were a significant part of the letter. In that case, mention them in the first paragraph.	I have enclosed two copies of the agreement. If you have comments, please call me between 2:00 and 4:00. Otherwise, I'll call Monday.
Proposals	End proposals of 10 pages or less simply by stating your final point. Your transition could be "Finally," or some other natural ending. For longer proposals, use a summary reminding the reader of the key benefits you'll provide.	In sum, Sommer and Caroll's programs will enhance your employees' spoken communications so they will have better customer relations, spend less time on the phone, and calm upset callers more easily.
Reports	For reports with a chronological order, simply end at the last event.	At 3:00 we left the scene and returned to the office.

	For other types of reports, include a conclusion.	These comments tell us that our customers are satisfied with all our services.
Bios	End bios with the least important—but interesting —experience or feature.	Mr. Collins was also in the 1996 *Who's Who in American Businesses.*
Press Releases	Always end a press release with a bio about you or your business and a line telling the reader where to go for more information.	Citizens interested in the Best Business program can call the mayor's hot line at 555-9292.

Summary or Conclusion: Lesser-Known Differences Between These Well-Known Endings

You probably know that many documents, such as white papers, articles, and proposals, end with summaries or conclusions. But you may not know that summaries and conclusions are different.

A summary does just what its name says: it summarizes your points. For 100-to-200-page pieces, place a summary after each major section. In 25-page white papers, place a summary at the end to remind your reader of key points. Be specific, too, since many readers flip to the summaries and leave the rest for another, never-to-be-seen, day.

Here's an example of a summary from a contractor's proposal:

As stated, we can offer your organization three distinct advantages:

1. The job will be finished in only two to three months depending on traffic and weather conditions.

2. Your bill will be 25% less with our company than with our competitors, since our specialists come from within our

organization rather than through outside contracting companies.

3. You'll receive monthly assessments for two years after the project is complete and can use our free call-in service five days a week if you have questions or concerns.

TRY THIS! Create strong openings and closings for the following documents:

1. You're writing a ten-page proposal about your recycling program for medium and large organizations, which consists of five steps: determining the most effective recycling plan according to the amount of paper your client uses and its hours of operation; setting up bins in key yet unobtrusive parts of the company; educating the employees about how to recycle and why; picking up the recyclables; billing the client. Your organization gives customers numerous advantages, including a competitive price for services, a flexible program, and 20 years' experience.

2. You're writing an information sheet about franchising opportunities for your bicycle shops. The sheet consists of two parts: (1) descriptions of the shops, including how the service area repairs broken bicycles and modifies new bikes, the 15 makes of mountain, racing, and touring bikes, and the apparel section; (2) instructions on how readers can apply for a franchise, which include filling out a complicated form with information about credit history and business experience.

3. You're writing a report based on an important company meeting, which you're sending to the parent organization. In the meeting, participants agreed that your organization is under-staffed, needs more backing for sales and marketing strategies and training programs, and must offer employees competitive wages. Otherwise, the organization will continue to lose money, offer an inferior product, and eventually collapse.

Conclusions draw a final point based on numerous other points. They must be interesting, important, specific, and tightly connected to the points before them. Seem hard? Not really. Just apply the same principles to your conclusions that you apply to all your writing. Here's another example from a contractor's proposal:

> Given these conditions, we can complete the job within two weeks for under $4,000—20% less than our competitors.

Beware: if your conclusion contains earth-shattering information, your reader may miss it. As always, play up your strongest points in the opening paragraph and refer to them as you go along.

TRY THIS! For a self-evaluation, write a detailed outline with three sections: your current responsibilities, your strengths, your weaknesses. Then, write the opening and closing paragraphs that give your readers the information you most want them to know and remember.

TROUBLESHOOTING

Just 500 Words More . . .

You've finished your document—an article for an important trade magazine. They wanted 2,000 words, you gave them, well, let's see . . . 1,500. Or you've created an information packet. You intended to create eight sheets for each of your company's services but, well, one service barely fills half a page. You go through your list, turning points like soil in a garden. But really—for once—you have nothing else to say. What do you do?

Easy. Consider the piece finished. After all, the idea that quantity means quality is as outdated as a manual typewriter. In fact, in the sound-bite mentality-era, long documents are detrimental. But, what if you really *must* produce more material? Then what? Here are a few suggestions.

Think graphics. Make sure your piece has an adequate amount of white space. Play with the design. Move your logo around. Experiment with photos and high-quality clip art. Most important, keep it professional and visually clean.

Think support. Interesting examples that support your point always help to add meat to the bone of your document. Take an information packet. For each service, add a few success stories from recent clients. And that article? Throw in a few examples or quotes.

Think devices. Now is your chance to be really creative. Add quotes to your information sheets, anecdotes set off from your main document, sidebars with lesser-known facts that will truly interest your readers. Perhaps you can add a "Did you know?" section, checklist, or other device to add flair—and words—to your article. Whatever else, do not repeat points, throw in extra words, or linger over minor points to squeeze extra words, sentences, or paragraphs into your once-strong document.

On the other hand, plenty of people have documents that are paragraphs or even pages too long. If this happens to you, simply cut the least important information. Down to your core idea? Cut any examples or other types of support.

And the Time Is . . .

Time, that nasty reality, claws and clings. And you dutifully want to revise for structure. Really. But you have to get that report to the boss's desk in 15 . . . 14 . . . 13 meager minutes. Wait—you still have enough time to edit. Simply determine which structural bad habit is most pronounced and edit for that. Are your openings dull? Check the first paragraph. Have trouble leading into examples? Double-check for transitions. This will improve your document while helping you hone your skills into professional quality.

CONCLUSION

Review every document for three important qualities: a powerful opening that grabs your readers' attention, a body that moves them from point to point without bumps or U-turns, and an ending that they'll value and remember. Once you have a solid structure, you can turn to the details that distinguish excellent writing.

Editing for Word Use

Object: *To locate and repair word-use problems in moments* while *improving your writing style.*

Creating strong word use is merely a matter of amending bad writing habits. This task is not as simple, or as difficult, as you may think.

Fortunately: You probably have fewer than five bad habits that infiltrate your style.

Unfortunately: They wander recklessly through every line you write, turning an otherwise strong message into mush.

Fortunately: Correcting these problems each time you rewrite will ultimately help you overcome them.

Unfortunately: You should focus on only one or two bad habits until you overcome them. Then tackle one or two more. This means that during the transition period, your documents will be better, but less than ideal.

Fortunately: If you write at least three times a week, you should overcome each problem in less than a month.

Unfortunately: You must first identify your bad habits, which can be as difficult as correcting them.

Fortunately: This chapter introduces a rewriting process that lets you quickly locate and correct your writing problems as you improve your skill.

To Grammar-check or Not to Grammar-check

In many ways, grammar-checks have become the darling of the computer age, alerting unsuspecting writers to passivity, among other hazards. Most programs even count the percentage of passives and provide scores, like an arcade game. Over 15 percent and you lose.

Are grammar-checks really helpful? Here are the pros and cons:

Pros: The computer quickly and easily points out problems in your writing style you didn't know existed. In some cases, the computer will make changes, saving you this minimal work.

Cons: To err is to be a computer—computers use a lot of valuable electricity being wrong. For the uncertain writer seeking advice about passives, this can be deadly. But, let's pretend computers *are* always right. Do you use a grammar-check? Go ahead, but don't rely on it. One of the biggest steps toward overcoming a problem is identifying it. Don't let the computer steal this valuable opportunity.

Your Bad Habits Are Invisible—To You!

Think of the associate who always interrupts—at meetings, social gatherings, or water-fountain chats. Or that vice president who shouts instead of talks. They are not aware of their bad habits. And you aren't about to point them out. Rather, you walk past their offices a little faster to avoid contact or end conversations a little sooner than necessary.

The parallel with writing is clear. You're unaware of the tired word use that makes your language as exciting as *Brady Bunch* reruns or the wordiness that adds pounds to every paragraph. But the problems are certainly there. Of course, your typical readers won't pick up your document and say, "Hum, this sentence is in the passive voice and ... uh-huh ... the tone of this article is pompous." But they'll have a vague, disturbing sense that the piece isn't worth reading, and they'll put it down.

When you speak to your readers later, of course, they won't say: "Gee, your letter was so poorly structured I couldn't get past the first paragraph," or, "I'm calling because your letter had too much jargon for me to understand." Instead, you exchange polite business conversation, neither of you mentioning your written work.

VISUAL EDITING: THE NO-READ APPROACH

Basically, two types of rewriters reign in the business world. Anal rewriters slowly read and reread every line, shifting words, shuffling paragraphs, then rereading the whole document again. They're perfectionists, never satisfied with the revision, yet never sure why. The other type, speedsters, are in a great hurry to get the piece out. They're confident, too, zooming through a document, changing a word, maybe two words, then sending the document out.

The plus side is that both types of writers attempt to rewrite. Both make two mistakes, though: (1) they reread their writing word by word (2) they edit for vague, undetectable problems.

Rather than use the approach of either type of rewriter, try the visual editing process. That's when you either skim your document or don't read it at all, but instead look for signs of one or two of your most extreme problems. For example, a symptom of wordiness is a pileup of little, extra words. If you see them, cut and rewrite the sentence. Have boring opening lines? Skim for tired phrases, your company name, "I" or "we."

If you diligently rewrite for a few weeks, narrowly seeking out one or two problems and correcting them, you'll notice two things:

1. Editing *really* is fast and easy—in fact, you do it automatically.

2. The problem shows up fewer times the next time you write. Soon, it rarely, if ever, crops up. Congratulations! You've overcome one bad habit. Now, move on to the next.

TRY THIS! For immediate benefit, read through the list of most common writing problems. Each time you review a problem in the book, check your writing samples. See it there? Great. You're infinitely closer to eliminating it than you were only moments before. So you don't forget, keep a list of your problems, determining which are constant and which only speckle your writing.

SPOTTING THE MOST COMMON PROBLEMS

The Business Community's Ten Most Prevalent Problems in Letter Composition

1. Passive voice
2. Wordiness
3. Tired phrases
4. Repeated words
5. Repeated ideas
6. Negative tone
7. General word use
8. Pompous tone
9. Boring sentence structure
10. Jargon

---

1. The Passive Voice

Signs: A helping verb, such as "was" or "had been," and often, but not always, a connecting word, such as "by" surrounding the action.

The contract *was* hit *by* the vice president.

What is the passive voice?

Perhaps the greatest roadblock to smooth, fast writing lies in sentence structure. Your reader wants to roll from point to point, the message as clear and unobstructed as cornfields in the Midwest.

But, serious accidents can happen along the way when you use the passive voice. One is convoluted or wordy language. Another, unclear sentences. A third, sentences with ambiguous actors—especially damaging in reports, proposals, and sales documents, where your organization most needs to take credit for their results.

Let's start by talking about the traditional *passive voice*, which you probably learned about in high school. Here's how it works. Every sentence must have two components: an actor and an action. Remember the first sentence you learned in grammar school? It probably involved Dick, Jane, and Spot, and they probably were running, talking, or engaging in some other basic activity:

actor	*action*
Jane	pats Spot.

Here, "Jane" is the actor and "pats" is the action. Spot, of course, receives the action. Most businesspeople get into trouble when they create the passive voice by separating the actor and action:

The proposal was reviewed by the committee.

"Committee" is the actor and "reviewed" is the action, yet they occupy separate ends of the sentence. This is like saying, "Spot is patted by Jane." To create a faster voice, simply reunite actor and action and cut a few words:

The committee reviewed the proposal.

Easy, right? But remember, before rewriting, you must distinguish the actor from other nouns. Take this passive sentence:

The information was faxed to Kilroy, Inc., on Friday by Ms. Danforth.

Here you have several nouns: "Friday," "Ms. Danforth," "information," and "Kilroy, Inc." Only one of these nouns, "Ms. Danforth," is the actor. The action is "faxed." The solution:

Ms. Danforth faxed the information to Kilroy, Inc., on Friday.

SAYING YES TO HELPING VERBS

Every year, I teach the passive-active idea to hundreds of people, from CEOs to engineers to secretaries. And every year a good percentage make this mistake: they believe that all helping verbs, regardless of context or use, indicate passivity. As a result, they edit out any sign of tense or degree, creating flat, grammatically dubious messages. So, *please* remember, connecting words and helping verbs are frequently important parts of an active, well-written message. Look at this example:

> We *had* discussed the first two sections of the proposal *by* the time Don Walsh arrived.

"We" is the actor and "discussed" is the action; "had" is a helping verb that shows when the action occurred in relation to Don Walsh's arrival. This sentence is passive-free.

Sometimes you can create passive writing by omitting the actor altogether, as in this example from a training manual:

> The seminars will be held in Conference Room B from 8:00 to 3:00, with a lunch break at noon.

The sentence contains an action, "held," yet no actor. Frequently when I discuss this problem in seminars, someone in the group protests: "The reader already knows who the actor is." True. But remember, by adding an actor you also create a faster, more direct message, containing those two vital components of any sentence— actor and action. Look at this revision:

> We will hold the seminars in Conference Room B from 8:00 to 3:00 with a lunch break at noon.

The I/We Phobia

One of the most glaring passive problems comes from a malady that plagues groups from outplacement firms to marketing departments—the I/we phobia. People feel that using the first person will take emphasis off the subject, make the message boring, or create

---

You and Me and Even I

One afternoon, a manager at a software development company showed me a stack of reports she'd written. The first thing I noticed was that she, like so many others in her organization, had strayed down the dreary path of passivity with writing like this:

> On Wednesday, DeltaTech was contacted so the next step to securing this important account could begin. Because the president was unavailable, her assistant was contacted and an appointment date was established.

As I expected, the manager was the actor in this actorless paragraph, but felt leery about using the dreaded "I." I gave her the first-person go-ahead, reinstating the importance of including an actor in every sentence. The next week, though, she returned with her revision. Here's the good news: she had created the active voice using clear, direct sentences. Now, the bad news: her message harbored enough pronouns to weigh down a computer screen.

> On Wednesday, I contacted DeltaTech so I could determine the next step I should take to secure this important account. I was unable to reach the president so I spoke with her assistant so I could arrange an appointment.

I explained that her revision needed some careful crafting. After all, she could create active language without repeating the actor. Eventually her well-written document looked like this:

> On Wednesday, I contacted DeltaTech to determine the next step in securing this important account. Since the president was unavailable, I spoke with her assistant to arrange an appointment.

unnecessary repetition. Let's set the record straight: *Yes*, you *can* use the first person. In fact, you need the first person when you or your organization is responsible for an action. You simply don't want to suffocate your writing with it.

Exceptions. Like most great rules, the rule against the passive voice has exceptions. In the newspaper business, for instance, reporters know that sometimes the recipient, or object, of the action is more interesting than the actor and belongs at the beginning of the sentence. For instance:

> Mayor Wilson was hit by a car.

In the active sentence, "A car hit Mayor Wilson," the actor, "car," is far less important than the recipient of the action, "Mayor Wilson."

In addition, the passive voice creates a smoother sentence when you have several actors:

> The proposal was developed by Tom Hutton of Craswell Industries, Lisa Glibb of LBG, Martin Hayes of Cantwell, Inc., and Fran Lincoln of GH Industries.

On a rare occasion, you will want to conceal the actor's identity, either because the circumstances are awkward or because you don't know the actor. A typical example is: "Fred was fired." Probably several individuals or an entire committee was responsible for firing Fred; you wouldn't want to mention any of them.

In addition, when you're giving your reader a command or an instruction, don't bother mentioning an actor. This device is a favorite of parents everywhere who use lines such as:

> Clean up that bedroom right now!

In the business world, speaking directly to the reader is helpful for creating tight, clear instructions for manuals, registration forms, and other documents. Here's an example from a training catalog:

To register for upcoming seminars, please:

- Print your name, department number, and extension number on the form below.
- Print the seminar number and name on the next line.
- Send this information to our office through interoffice mail by January 21.
- Be sure to arrive at the seminars at least ten minutes before the official starting time.

Imagine that each one of these commands has a "you" hidden within it that the reader naturally anticipates and understands.

Secrets of the Passive Voice Revealed!

Rumor: *Passive* means boring words; *active* means lively words.

Truth: Passive and active voice address a *structural* issue only—the relationship between the actor and the action in the sentence.

Rumor: Sometimes no one is responsible for the action.

Truth: This idea defies every scientific notion imaginable. A leaf is blown around. What blew the leaf? The wind. A child is frightened in the night but no one and nothing lurks in the room. Something imaginary scared the child.

Rumor: If you want to be secretive, use passives.

Truth: Nope. If you want to be secretive, omit information—an entirely different idea from omitting an actor. Don't say, "The assignment was carried out." Say, "One of our team carried out the assignment."

Rumor: The reader doesn't know the difference between passive and active, so why worry?

Truth: Right, the reader *doesn't* know the difference between passive and active. Or between a misplaced modifier and a logical sentence. Or, for that matter, between one grammatical idea and another. *But*, the reader will become confused and distracted by passives, so avoid them.

TRY THIS! Test your rewriter's eye by locating the passive voice.

1. Review your notes to make sure that behavioral observations are stated and are not arbitrary judgments. These reviews will be examined by the committee and used to evaluate the employee. If there are any concerns, please contact me. It is important that all your questions are answered before the report is completed.

2. Some of the information that will be learned is how to ask the right questions to gauge customer satisfaction and how to read data so that important insights can be gained. The groups are deliberately kept small so participants can raise individual concerns and cases. To participate, a check for $150 per person should be received by February 15. Our staff can be contacted at extension 1232 if more information is needed.

2. Wordiness

Signs: Excessive use of little words.

Remember that floor-cleaning ad of years ago? The one with an announcer informing homemakers everywhere that their floors were suffering from dull, waxy buildup? As businesspeople, you must confront a similar problem: unsightly little-word buildup, which collects on the page and dulls the smooth, sparkling finish of your message. Worse, it confuses your readers and makes a potentially interesting message boring. And nothing distracts today's impatient readers as much as that. The solution: cut the little-word buildup.

Four Simple Steps to Wipe Away Little-Word Buildup

Use this approach and after only a few weeks, cutting extra words should become a tidy, one-minute process for your average letter:

1. *Look for clusters of two-, three-, and four-letter words and boring, unnecessary words.* Basically, think small. Sometimes these

PIT STOP

Do and Don't

When making a document concise:

Do: Cut extra, unnecessary words that weigh down the message.

Don't: Deliberately keep a document short, randomly slash words to shrink a paragraph, omit necessary details and vital descriptive words, or cut support material. A 500-page detailed scientific analysis can be concise, while a 3-paragraph cover letter can be wordy.

little words may hide between substantive words. Sometimes not. Here's an example:

> The team planned to go to the meeting that will be held on Friday at a little before 10:00.

2. *Circle or highlight these words.* This will heighten your awareness of little-word buildup, and help you revise quickly.

> The team planned to <u>go to the</u> meeting <u>that will be held on</u> Friday <u>at a little</u> before 10:00.

3. *Cut and create tighter sentences.* Now, simply lift the wordiness off the page. Occasionally you may add one strong word to replace several weak ones. No, you shouldn't use seventeen-syllable replacements, which intimidate and bore the average reader. Go for ordinary, clean words, which your reader can glide across like a skater over ice. The revision:

> The team planned to attend Friday's meeting just before 10:00.

4. *Compare the number of words in your first and second versions.* This will help you identify little-word buildup and, eventually,

cut little words *before* you write them. In the last example, we moved from 19 words to 12 words—a 36 percent savings in readers' time.

What constitutes an unsightly little word? Prepositions, articles, conjunctions, and other small words that hide between larger ones, in cracks between sentences, and in spaces between thoughts like verbal fleas. Also, those two- and three-letter words that cluster together throughout a document. Longer, flat, and equally unnecessary words may join them. Look at this example from an in-house memo:

> In today's meeting, we were happy to have the opportunity to welcome John Spaulding. He reviewed some of the newest types of evaluations. If you have any questions about these evaluations, feel free to call him at the education center. (42 words)

Some of the extra words are:

> were happy to have the opportunity to
>
> some of the
>
> any
>
> about these evaluations
>
> feel free to

Now, look at the improved version:

> In today's meeting, we welcomed John Spaulding, who reviewed new types of evaluations. If you have questions, call him at the education center. (23 words)

Some people take an instinctive approach to repairing their message once the extra words are gone, juggling around the pieces until the sentence sounds right. This method has a creative quality, much like a jazz player who can't read music and doesn't understand music theory, but finds the melody by feel. The trick is to make sure your revisions are *improvements,* not merely changes.

Tighten, Tighten, Tighten

Notice the difference between these wordy and tight phrases:

Instead of	*Write*
As head of the department, she was able to . . .	As department head . . .
We received your letter that was dated July 16.	We received your July 16 letter.
We completed the manual that was long and difficult.	We completed the long, difficult manual.
This is the new system that MIS developed.	This is MIS's new system.

3. Tired Phrases

Signs: Clusters of overused and wordy phrases.

Those dull, tired phrases. The trouble is that most businesspeople think they are necessary—even professional—and sneak them into their writing. Some businesspeople even claim they're the only option in a world with all too few words.

I recently worked with the marketing department at a large insurance company. The writers could string words together like beads on a necklace. Besides that, they were energetic, spending nine or ten hours writing under deadline with barely a complaint. However, one writing quirk guaranteed that their newsletters, brochures, and announcements would end up in the trash. Tired expressions relegated their otherwise peppy and informative language into dreary smears of words. We reviewed lines like these:

> You can always be sure that our coverage will give you the protection you want day in and day out.

> At our insurance company, we do our best to provide you with the services that will meet your needs.

They tried writing and rewriting, each time coming up with dull and wordy expressions. At last, the vice president, who sat among the group, said, "You have to use these phrases—there's no choice!"

Untrue! For every wordy, tired phrase, you can find a fresh or, simply, more direct one. This example:

> You can always be sure that our coverage . . .

can become:

- Be assured our coverage
- Just know our coverage
- Naturally our coverage

Reminder: Use Care and Judgment When Cutting!

You do want to wring extra words from your writing like water from a sponge. And you do want the fastest, liveliest language possible. But you must use care and logic when making corrections, as this cautionary tale reveals:

> Several years ago, I trained the workforce at a manufacturing company, starting with the senior managers and moving to other levels. As I was discussing the importance of using tight, concise language, one of the managers stopped me to explain that several years before, another writing consultant had trained his department's employees. He had emphasized, as I did, the problem of wordiness. Everyone loved the seminar and walked away with improved writing skills.
>
> So they had thought. According to the manager, once the employees returned to their desks and actually started writing, their messages were weaker than before. The problem was so intense that management essentially had to *un*train them! After working with his employees in subsequent sessions, I understood why. They were trying so hard to eliminate extra words, they chopped out information that would support them in court or explain touchy decisions about broken parts or prices.

> . . . will give you the protection you want . . .

can become:

- will protect you
- will give you vital protection
- will give you appropriate protection

> . . . day in and day out

can become:

- always
- constantly
- ceaselessly

The idea, again, is to cut ho-hum phrases and replace them with simpler, more direct alternatives. You can use a different tone, too, creating a less wordy, more saleslike message:

> At our insurance company, we do our best to provide your family with the coverage that will meet all your needs

can become:

- Getting your family the right coverage—that's your goal and our business.
- Like a carpenter, we work to build your family the sturdiest, most reliable coverage possible.

Now, look at this paragraph from a chiropractor's office:

> I am writing again in regard to your visits to our office. As I previously mentioned in our last letter, in spite of the fact that you promised to pay in full on numerous other occasions, we have not received any payments. In view of this fact, we must refuse to provide further treatments at this point in time. If you do not send a payment as soon as possible, we must forward your account to our legal department.

By cutting tired phrases, this document can look like this:

> As I mentioned in my last letter, we have not received any payments from you, although you promised to pay for your chiropractic visits in full. Therefore, we must withhold further treatments. If you do not send a payment immediately, we must forward your account to our legal department.

Ah, Those Run-Down Phrases

Notice the difference between these wordy and concise phrases:

Wordy	Concise
in the event that	if
do not hesitate to contact me at once	contact me immediately
in the near future	soon
the means by which	how
in view of the fact that	because
it will not be possible for us to	we cannot
in a state of change	changing
as a result of	because of
it is certainly true that	true
have the capability of	can
not only . . . but	both
during the course of the year	throughout the year
in regard to	regarding
in view of the fact that	since
at this point in time	currently
in spite of the fact that	although
numerous occasions	often
as soon as possible	soon, immediately
it is necessary for us to	we must
we are able to	we can
a range of your requirements	your requirements
in addition to	also

How do you identify tired expressions? As always, the little words are a tip-off. Look for them. In addition, consciously seek out phrases you've seen over and over, then cut. Finally, listen to your sentences. If you notice a dull, constant rhythm, check your word use.

4. Repeated Words

Signs: Words repeated four or five times in an average paragraph or three or more times in a sentence.

Businesspeople typically pound repeated words, phrases, lines, paragraphs, and even complete ideas into their writing, stretching a two-minute message into what seems like hours. Redundancy is more than an unfortunate habit, however, and results from four factors:

1. The first, most deadly factor, is insecurity. If you say it once, well, that's okay, but are you *really* being clear enough? After all, the offer is so good or the instructions are so complicated, you must describe every important nuance. Sometimes this process is barely conscious—the repeats just slip in, filling up the page. The simple alternative: say it once and say it right, then move to the next point.

2. Many businesspeople feel a subtle but ever-present mistrust of their readers. They think they *need* to pound their message into their readers' brains. After all, readers might be dull witted or perhaps lazy, and they probably watch so much TV they can't possibly absorb the message the first time through. Some of this may be true. On the other hand, your readers might be bright and fully conscious of what they are reading. Make sure your message *hops*, not *drags*, by cutting redundancy.

3. Rather than vary sentence structure, shift the actor, play with transitions, or dig up alternative words, some writers repeat the same words and phrases as a way to glue the message together. Structurally, anyway, this trick works. Yet the message seems as foundationless and flimsy as a child's paper house. To create great writing, tattoo this word into your thoughts: *variety.*

4. The notion of repetition is based on the surprisingly solid, yet misleading, idea that to drive a message home, you must remind the reader of your main point or points. It's *true* when you're writing 90-page theses, 500-page dissertations, and 300-page proposals. But repetition only bogs down your average 1-to-5-page letters, brochures, case studies, reports, and other documents.

Of all the poor writing habits, repeated words are probably the easiest to detect. Simply look for words that appear approximately three or more times in a paragraph and cut. Take this typical example, the repeated "I" from a cover letter to a potential employer:

> I currently earn a salary in the low six figures. I would consider opportunities at this level.

To eliminate the "I," combine sentences:

> I currently earn a salary in the low six figures and would consider opportunities at this level.

If you really want a smooth finish, you can cut even further:

> I would consider opportunities at my current, low-six-figure level.

This strategy usually works when you have one actor involved in two or three short actions. More often, one person, organization, or item is involved in numerous actions for several paragraphs or pages. The best solution: Shift the focus onto a different actor. Here's an example:

> Our alarm <u>system</u> offers a 24-hour security guard who signals the police at the slightest suggestion of an intruder. Our *system* also offers something other <u>systems</u> don't: a backup response unit in case of electrical failure. Our <u>system</u> also contains the newest computerized scanning device that determines exactly where and when the intrusion occurred.

Now, shift the focus to the person who matters most: the reader. In the process, you'll replace that repeated "system" with more interesting language:

> With our alarm system, you'll have a 24-hour security guard who signals the police at the suggestion of an intruder. You'll also appreciate the computerized scanning device that determines exactly where and when the intrusion occurred. No need to worry about electrical failure, either, thanks to our backup response unit.

Another option most business writers love is bullets:

> Our alarm system is unique because it gives you:
>
> - A 24-hour security guard who signals the police at the slightest suggestion of an intruder.
> - A backup response unit so you're always protected— even with electrical failure.
> - The newest computerized scanning device to determine exactly where and when the intrusion occurred.

A word of caution here. One of the most common repetition problems appears in bullets with setups like this:

> **Why use Quick-Clean services?**
>
> - We are knowledgeable. That means we know your business's needs—whether a small office or a large warehouse.
> - We are also experienced. In fact, we have 50 long years of experience making business environments sparkling clean.
> - We make sure our staff is trained to polish every surface and clean every corner.

And this:

Professional Printers will give you:

- a unique selection of paper products
- a trained staff who will help you develop a look that's right for your business
- a 10% discount the first time you use our service

Starting each bullet with the same words is fatal to the fast, clean message both writers intended. Look at these revisions:

Why use Quick-Clean services? Here are three good reasons:

- **Knowledge.** We know your business needs—whether a small office or a large warehouse.
- **Experience.** For almost 50 years, we've made businesses sparkling clean.
- **Training.** All our staff receive training on effective ways to polish every surface and clean every corner.

Professional Printers will give you a:

- unique selection of paper products
- trained staff who will help you develop a look that's right for your business
- 10% discount the first time you use our service

Exceptions: Repetition *can* work in your favor. Like a good dance beat, it keeps readers going, moving them from point to point in a jouncy, suggestive style. Here's an example from an in-house memo at an accounting firm:

> Yes, our processes need to be faster. And yes, Ted's idea about restructuring the managerial team will have many benefits. And yes, giving Jeff the Candice account will free up Mike and Terry. But you can take an easier, more streamlined approach to making these changes.

When using repetition, do so consciously, and follow these guidelines:

- Use repetition only once in a two- or three-page document. The novelty of any unusual format or style vanishes pretty quickly.
- Repeat interesting words that will intrigue your readers. Scratch small, everyday words, such as "we," or phrases, such as "we can help you," from the list.
- Reinforce your organization's image or your primary message in whichever word or phrase you repeat. Interesting buzzwords that appear throughout your document will work well here.
- Introduce repeated words or phrases at the beginning of a sentence or paragraph when possible, so they act as hooks, taking your readers from thought to thought.

5. Repeated Ideas

Signs: This habit is difficult to spot immediately. Read through your document, deliberately looking for repeated ideas. Find any? If so, check every document you write for several weeks to correct and ultimately eliminate this problem.

With this second redundancy problem, repeated meaning, you repeat the message using different words. In the following example, the writer thought he was creating lively language, but he was also added unnecessary words:

> At Visual Corporation, Sheila Bently served as Vice President of Administration and Planning. In this capacity, she managed 200 functions a year.

"In this capacity" and "Vice President of Administration and Planning" say the same thing. This revision works better:

> As Vice President of Administration and Planning at Visual Corporation, Sheila Bently managed over 200 functions a year.

Mending this problem takes more than a quick cut and paste. In most cases, you need to break down and combine your sentences, tossing away words as you do. Look at these instances of repetition and their word-saving solutions.

> Direct mail pieces play a critical role in marketing campaigns. By using this type of sales technique, you provide a quick, timely message that the prospective customers can easily read and appreciate. Numerous other documents can be helpful in your campaign to reach as many potential customers as possible.

becomes:

> Direct-mail pieces, among other documents, play a critical role in marketing campaigns by providing a quick, timely

---

Common (for most people?!) Business Writing Redundancies

absolutely complete	basic fundamentals
follows after	reduce down
free and clear	refer back
cease and desist	full and complete
repeat again	collect together
future plans	return back
true and correct	important essentials
very unique	integral part
enclosed herewith	end result
actual truth	completely false
entirely complete	alter or change
and then	personal opinion
my own	important necessity
final outcome	assemble together
midway between	vitally essential
old patterns	each and every

TRY THIS! Isolate and cut the wordiness in these paragraphs.

> Each year, on January 1, thousands of people make resolutions to welcome in the new year. And every year, thousands of people break their new resolutions—especially when they resolve to stop smoking completely. For this reason, among many others, our company and numerous other companies have absolutely resolved to make the entire month of January a no-smoking month.
>
> If you see a fellow employee engaged in a smoking activity, tell that person you care and then ask him or her to put the cigarette out. If you are a smoker, you can go to our nurses' station where you will receive free candy and gum to help you stop smoking cigarettes. These treats are free and are available to all smokers in our company during this no-smoking month.
>
> The no-smoke campaign is an integral part of the company's Live Well campaign that includes sports activities, diet tips for weight loss, and more!

> message that prospective customers can easily read and appreciate.

This:

> An important part of our company's purpose is to develop housing solutions that are environmentally sensitive. To accomplish this very important goal, we understand both the law regarding environmental regulations and its purpose.

becomes:

> One of our missions is to develop environmentally sensitive housing solutions by understanding the relevant laws and the purposes behind them.

Sometimes redundancy lurks in sets of words that repeat, rather than reinforce, meaning. For example, "past history." If future history were possible, we'd all take Future History 101 and learn which stock to pick in the year 2030. Another example is "sports activities," as in "The YMCA likes to encourage teens to participate in sports activities." Sports *is* an activity, so cut.

6. Negative Tone

Signs: Negative words, such as "not" and negating words, such as "possibly" and the prefix "un."

Positive writing is an important way to create a strong relationship with your readers and deliver bad news as effectively as possible. This does not mean that you will sound like Pollyanna, pretending the sun is shining during a storm. Rather, you will create a strong, forward-looking tone that is realistic and convincing. In fact, the ideas governing the positive voice would make great material for a how-to book on marriage. Just look:

- Avoid negating words, such as "just," "unfortunately," "may," "might," "possibly," and "perhaps."

    In the business world, a line like this:

    > The Forester Company might possibly offer the best customer service in the state.

    will sound more convincing with a positive slant:

    > The Forester Company provides some of the best customer service in the state.

    This line:

    > Unfortunately, Nina Dow, our Executive Vice President, is leaving the company on November 15 after 12 years.

sounds better this way:

> Nina Dow, our Executive Vice President, will be leaving after 12 successful years with our company.

• Avoid apologizing too profusely.

In the business world you want to be honest in your correspondences and admit your organization's mistakes. But honesty doesn't mean you need to dwell on the negative aspect of the situation or apologize on bended knee. Focus on the changes your company made once it became aware of the situation.

Rather than write:

> We are terribly sorry that our representative was abrupt on the telephone last Tuesday. This is inexcusable behavior and we were shocked to hear of it.

Write:

> Thank you for informing us that our representative was abrupt on the telephone last Tuesday. We spoke with her, and she sends her apologies and assures us that she will not use that tone again.

• Avoid negative words that leave writing vague and indirect.

In business documents you can simply cut out negatives, such as "no," "not," and "not only," from your writing and replace them with more specific and direct alternatives.

Instead of this line:

> Not only should you complete and mail the form, but you should send us $200 for dues.

Write this one:

> Please complete and send the form with $200 for dues.

By using positive language, you also create an opportunity to become more specific, and in the process, more lively and informative.

Accentuate the Positive

Your significant other wants you to take the weekend off. After all, you've been working weekends for a month on that loathsome proposal your team *still* hasn't finished. And, really, you want to take the weekend off. And maybe you can. If not Saturday, maybe Sunday. Maybe. If you say, "I might be able to get some time off," your partner's expression will drop into one suitable for a bulldog. Try, "I can only take Sunday," and he looks betrayed. But say, "I'll try really hard. At the very least, we'll have Sunday," and your partner's heart starts beating a love song.

Apology Exaggerated

You had a fight that morning, something about a vacation and how she wanted to spend it on a golf course while you were hoping for a trip abroad. You raised your voice, okay, and that was wrong. But both of you were late for work, the kids were shouting, and the pressure was sizzling. When you get home, you apologize with a "Oh honey, I'm sorry." She understands. Add a little more apology: "Honey, I'm sorry, I don't know what the problem is. I was just so terrible. Please forgive me." Now she's agreeing. You were terrible and, by the way, do you remember how you spoke to her last week? A little more apology, and she acknowledges that the level of the affront is astounding. You endure a tense, all-night silence not even a new infusion of apology can relax.

The Power of Positive Wording

You're heading for a formal dinner. Your partner is dressed in tux and tie. Shoes shiny. Hair slicked back. He looks in the mirror three, no, four, no, five times. When he asks how he looks, better not respond with "Not too bad," or "Not undesirable." Try "great," "gorgeous," "sexy," or about a hundred other positive adjectives first.

This line:

> This is not the same packet we sent you last week.

would be more reader friendly this way:

> This is a new, more comprehensive packet.

And:

> This is not the best bid.

is stronger when written this way:

> This bid is 25% more expensive and they'll take two months longer than the other contractors.

• Place good news first.

Remember, good news creates a good mood. If you have a reason to thank your reader, for example, start with that. If you are responding to a complaint, thank the reader for contacting you about the problem.

Instead of this line:

> Although we cannot send you the full amount you requested, we will reinstate your policy with no charge.

How Was Your Day?

My friend and her spouse bought a new car, a new house, and new furniture. In short, they were broke. Then, one glorious afternoon, they received a $500 tax-return check. Unfortunately, that glorious afternoon grew dim just a few hours later when their refrigerator died, never to revive. The day brightened a little again, though, when my friend learned that a replacement would cost $500. That night she told her spouse: "We just got a $500 tax return. And guess what? The refrigerator died, but we don't have to worry since the $500 will cover it." Her spouse was delighted.

---

use this one:

> We will gladly reinstate your policy with no charge and can reimburse you for $52 of the amount you requested.

Positive Power. Another reason why the positive voice makes such a surprising and refreshing change: 75 percent of our daily conversations focus on negative subjects.

Exceptions: Perhaps you are involved in legislative work, fund-raising, or some other activity that fights for a cause or against one. In these cases, you can highlight the negative to alert the reader to the severity of the issue:

TRY THIS! Yes, you can make the following negative statements positive:

1. We mistakenly sent you the wrong form requesting information about your family. Please throw this card away and complete the enclosed card instead. This information is vital for our files. We truly regret any inconvenience this mistake caused you. Like most organizations, we rely on automation to help us increase efficiency and responsiveness to our clients. Unfortunately, even the best systems make mistakes. Again, please accept our apologies. We hope that you continue to do business with us.

2. Please accept our apologies for taking so long to send the materials that you requested. We are unable to keep up with the demands of the public and have been backlogged for several weeks. If you do not find all the information you need here, or have any questions or concerns, please call. If I do not answer the phone personally, don't hesitate to leave a message and I will call you back not too long after.

> In the United States, one of every five children is hungry. And, with diminishing funds going into school-lunch and after-school programs, more will join the list.

You may attempt to be starkly one-sided to elicit a response. Here are two examples:

> Two employees left this month and two the month before. Yet the company hasn't filled these positions. As a result, we're seriously understaffed and have a growing backlog of work.

and:

> Jerry O'Connor arrives at least an hour late every day. He is so rude that three employees have written complaints against him. In addition, he gets reports in late, if at all. I have documented these matters in greater detail in the enclosed report.

7. General Word Use

Signs: Strings of flat, common words.

Let's take another look at your average reader. Most likely this person is inundated with reading material at work and at home. For relaxation, he or she watches TV and reads *TV Guide*—the second most popular publication in the United States, with a circulation of 14,037,062. Consider this movie listing from that magazine:

> Cult filmmaker John Waters's mainstream homage to the harried housewife (played by transvestite Divine).

In business writing, you must compete with this type of language without being flashy or cute. After all, you're trying to provide information or get a response, not host MTV. A vitally important way to achieve your goal is through specific word use. Notice the specifics in the *TV Guide* blurb: "cult," "mainstream,"

"harried," "played by transvestite," "Divine." With general words
the language dies:

> Filmmaker John Waters's homage to housewives.

Now look at the *TV Guide*'s farcical take on the "Flubs & Fumbles" of football:

> At a Saturday evening charity banquet, Rapunzel-tressed
> Carolina Panthers' linebacker Kevin Greene finds himself seated
> at a table with smoldering sex object Fabio, who is wearing a
> clone of Greene's "one-of-a-kind" Armani tux.

And see the difference in this general rendition:

> At a charity dinner, the Carolina Panthers' Kevin Greene sat
> beside Fabio, who was wearing the same tux.

Notice the difference between this general sentence from a training manual discussing an upcoming computer-skills seminar:

> Computers have helped Olympic Food's employees write better
> letters faster.

and the specific revision:

> Computers have helped Olympic Food's employees write
> grammatically superior letters three times faster than 20
> years ago.

Why Specifics? A Reason with Teeth

Suppose I told you my friend was attacked by a dog. What would you
envision? Chances are a gray, nondescript blur of motion. Now, what
if I told you that my friend was attacked by a German shepherd? You
would have a clear image of a huge bulk of fur and teeth lunging for a
person's neck. On the other hand, if I said my friend was attacked by a
Chihuahua, you'd see a tiny, trembling creature attached to someone's
pant leg. Specific words such as "Chihuahua" and "German shepherd"
create a concrete and unmistakably different set of images.

Such words as "three times" and "grammatically" are more interesting than "better" and "more." They also demonstrate the specific degree of improvement. Rather than say, "In addition to saving you money, our discount plan gives you numerous advantages," say, "In addition to saving you money, our discount plan gives you these six advantages." Then, set up a clean list that your readers can quickly anticipate and follow.

Another advantage to specifics: they make your writing objective, rooting your statements in fact rather than in opinion. For example, this line is purely opinion:

> We are the most popular health club in Greenville County.

After all, popularity is a vague, unmeasureable idea. By being specific, you provide the reader with believable information:

> We have 2,000 members—more than any other health club in Greenville County.

Similarly, this general statement:

> We tried calling you numerous times to clarify this matter.

would be more credible if specific:

> We tried contacting you on Monday and Tuesday mornings to discuss your account.

Creating a specific message doesn't necessarily mean you must create a longer one. You can often substitute one word for one or two others, as in these examples:

General	Specific
expensive	fits five comfortably
soon	Monday
nice	generous
helpful	prompt
expensive	$20,000

better	cleaner
fast	by 2:00
difficult	complex
reader	member
a lot	30%
late	weeks overdue
bigger	fits five comfortably
small	1%
old	since 1910

Exceptions: For legal reasons, you can't use specifics in some materials, particularly in sales and marketing pieces. Your company's legal department should have helpful guidelines.

The Right Time for Specifics

Be sure to use specifics when you're mentioning

Times: The meeting began at 1:00 and ended at 1:10.

Dates: I will contact you on July 15 to confirm our plans for the following morning.

Money: With the merger, we should gross $2.5 million more than last year.

Figures: Twenty percent of our customers live in Colorado Springs.

Identities: Martin Manson, publisher of the *Brownsville Star*, will support George Frank for mayor.

Descriptions: All our clothing is made from 100% cotton or wool.

Actions: Our company developed a 200-page assessment of National Bank's managerial practices.

Benefits: Our remodeling service will transform your reception area in less than a month for only $20,000: half our competitor's fee.

8. Pompous Tone

Signs: Large—and unnecessary—million-dollar words. Also, jargon and passives.

Tone is the way you communicate to someone. For example, if you were to walk into a room full of screaming children, you'd probably say something like this:

> Everyone sit down and be quiet this minute.

If you were to walk into a board meeting you'd more likely say something like this:

> Could everyone please sit down? We'd like to start the meeting.

Tone is also one of your best public relations tools, establishing your organization's personality. How do you create an appropriate tone, one that is friendly and professional? Pretend that the reader is standing by your desk. If this person has a professional demeanor, you're not going to say, "Hi, how the heck are ya?" Rather, you'll say, "It's nice to meet you in person." On the other hand, if this person is angry, you would calm him or her by saying, "Please tell me the problem," rather than, "What do you want?"

How do you say it?

Your tone generally falls somewhere in this range:

Pompous: Overly formal, often contains passivity and jargon. Many businesspeople mistake the pompous tone for a professional one and use it regularly.

Professional: Relaxed, reader focused yet businesslike. Good for letters, memos, reports, proposals, and some newsletter articles.

Informal: Conversational. Good for sales and marketing materials and some letters.

Although your documents do not adhere strictly to one tone, they probably sound something like one of these:

Pompous

Dear Mr. Smith:

Enclosed please find the information that was requested in our telephone communication of May 14. As was mentioned at that time, Midville Hospital has significantly more doctors of exceptional quality than any other health facility in the state.

As you were also informed, our organization has offices located throughout the state. In the event that you need a specialist, our professionals will refer you to the most appropriate party. You are also entitled to utilize one of our numerous programs that will assist you and your family in achieving the highest level of health possible.

Please contact me in the event that you have questions or would like additional information.

Most sincerely yours,

Professional

Dear Mr. Smith,

I am sending along the information you requested on Friday. As I mentioned, Midville Hospital has more doctors than any hospital in the state.

In addition, we have a vast network of doctors and other health professionals with offices throughout Massachusetts and in parts of New Hampshire and Rhode Island. If you need a specialist, they can refer you to the right one. You and your family can also participate in numerous programs such as smoking-cessation classes, a 24-hour hotline with a registered nurse to answer your questions seven days a week, health fairs, and more.

Feel free to call anytime between 9:00 and 5:00 Monday through Friday if you would like more information.

Sincerely,

Informal

Dear Bob—

Just sending along the information we talked about Friday. As I said, Midville Hospital has more doctors than any hospital in the state. We also have an impressive network of doctors and other professionals with offices near your work or home. Need a specialist? They'll refer you to the right one. You and your family can also get health-wise thanks to our numerous programs designed to help you quit smoking or improve your overall fitness. We even have a health hotline designed to answer your health questions all day every day.

Want to know more? Just call. I'm at the office between 9:00 and 5:00, Monday through Friday.

Take care!

Here are some words to watch for when you're checking tone:

Pompous	*Conversational*
accompany	go with
accordingly	so
aforementioned	these, the
appeared to be	seemed
attributable	due
by means of	by
compensate	pay
considerable	large
correspondence	letter
facilitate	help
foregoing	this, these

furthermore	also, in addition
inasmuch as	because
indebtedness	debt
indicate	show
informed	told
in order to	to
in the event that	if
numerous	many
possessed	had
prior to	before
provided that	if
purchase	buy
similar to	like
stated	said
terminate	end
utilize	use
visualize	see
whether or not	whether
with regard to	about

Three Million Readers Can't Be Wrong

Even though you shouldn't write in a newspaper tone, *Newsweek* provides the kind of writing your reader wants—its circulation is 3,158,617. Look at this leading article from *Newsweek*'s business section:

> Guys, it's your turn. As women are liberated from some of the meaner dictates of dress, men are losing a certain brand of fashion freedom. Sure, you may no longer have to wear a suit and tie to work. But there's the rub. With so many offices gone "casual," the corporate uniform is gone. You have to consider not only when to dress up or down, but a whole new vocabulary of texture, pattern and fabric.

Exceptions: There are no exceptions. The pompous tone is alienating, boring, and outdated. On the other hand, the professional and informal tones are *not* interchangeable. For example, if you're sending employees a memo about internal changes, use the professional tone. Sending an information sheet? Determine which tone is best for your product or service. Sending an invitation to a fund-raising celebration? Keep it relaxed.

9. Boring Sentence Structure

Signs: Sentences of approximately the same length.

Which is true? The average sentence length should be:

a. between one and one-and-a-half lines
b. up to three lines
c. one line, unless it contains a list, then three lines is okay
d. none of the above
e. all of the above

The answer: e. all of the above. Ideally you should vary your sentence length, establishing a rhythm for your writing. This paragraph sounds flat:

> Shut off the lights and lock the door if you are the last person to leave the office at night. Also, tell the security guard the office is empty so he can set the alarm. Tell him to shut it off if you need to return to the office.

Now, note the rhythmic difference in the next paragraph, which uses a variety of sentences but states the same message:

> When you're the last one leaving the office, always shut off the lights, lock the door, and tell the security guard the office is empty. He'll set the alarm. Need to return to the office? Tell him to shut it off again.

The sounds of writing

You may not hear violins, but writing has its own music. Some documents move quickly, with numerous short lines and repetitions. Others move slowly, developing ideas in a few long sentences then elaborating with bullets. The rhythmic difference between documents can be as extreme as the difference between an African drumbeat and a waltz. When you're writing well, your readers will—consciously or not—hear it. The best tools for constructing a flowing melody or a startling beat are these.

Short–long–short–long sentences. A great way to set up an interesting, even dynamic, rhythm, is by juxtaposing short and long sentences. This device is great for marketing pieces, in which the musicality of the language creates a background for the message. But it's also great for instructions, opinion pieces, argumentative letters, and even questionnaires:

> You stated that BellTech, Inc., owed you back pay for vacation time. Not true. Contractors are not entitled to paid vacation time. You also stated that we owed you for extra hours—up to 60 per week. This, too, is untrue. You volunteered to stay. In fact, our managers specifically requested that you leave at 4:00 every day, repeatedly stating that your weekly pay would not increase.

Unusual punctuation. Most people stick with basic punctuation marks: commas, periods, and question marks when appropriate. But play around a little, using colons, dashes, semicolons, and ellipses—among others. Here are a few examples:

> Food has always been the key factor at any successful fund-raising event.

is more lively when written like this:

> One factor is always key at any successful fund-raising event: food.

Similarly, this typical line:

> Wonderland Toys carries bicycles, sleds, board games, swing sets, and more!

has more personality like this:

> Bicycles, sleds, board games, and swing sets—Wonderland Toys carries all that and more!

And, you can write everyday messages like these:

> John Robertson discussed the industry's changing image. He's an expert because his company has been researching the subject for years.

this way:

> John Robertson discussed the industry's changing image; his company has been researching the subject for years.

Questions. Most likely, you use questions only at the beginning of a document, if at all. Questions are a great way to punch up your writing. For starters, readers hear questions differently from other sentences. Also, you can use one, three, six, ten, or any number of words to form a question, unlike other types of sentences. Finally, questions stop the motion of your writing while the answer starts it up again, establishing a nice rhythm:

> Jane Fisherman is an excellent employee who fully deserves the Employee of the Year Award. Why? The answer is simple. She understands every aspect of her position and is results driven.

Incomplete sentences. The great taboo. Incomplete sentences. The ones every grammar-check program tells us about and every editor eyes distrustfully. But incomplete sentences *do* have their place, especially when you're accentuating a point. Just be sure to use incomplete sentences consciously and wisely, so your readers get absorbed in your message and don't pause, thinking you made a grammatical mistake:

> In the woods on a sunny afternoon. Thoughtful. Relaxed. Silence surrounding you. Sound like a good dream? Actually, it's this year's managers' retreat at the Northern Hills Conference Center.

Sentences beginning with "and" and "but." Here's another great taboo. *And*, yes, you can begin sentences with "and" and "but" as long as your thoughts flow smoothly. In fact, these words break the sentence rhythm, placing emphasis on the words that follow. Here are a few examples:

> At Hollow Crest Farms, we produce the best goat cheese and sheep's milk anywhere. But just as important, we deliver it fresh every day. And that means superior taste and quality for our customers.

Exceptions: Although you should always vary your sentences, be aware of how sentence length and structure affect your tone. For example, colons joining two interrelated sentences make the tone more formal, while dashes make it more relaxed.

10. Jargon

Signs: Strings of long, industry-related words, abbreviations, and acronyms.

Jargon refers to words individuals in specific industries use to describe their services or products. The high-tech industry, for example, is loaded with jargon. So is the financial world.

When you see jargon from other industries, you probably get confused and distracted, wanting familiar terms instead. On the other hand, your organization's jargon probably seems natural to you. But, it will alienate your readers, causing them to skim your document or put it away altogether. By using more natural language you'll create a more inviting message. This does not mean that you'll lower your standard of writing or sound less professional. Nor does it mean that you'll develop one writing style for all audiences. And yes, you can still use words specific to your field, such as the names of processes or parts.

Look at the difference between jargon and relaxed language in the following examples:

A Legal Letter

Jargon: In response to your 93A demand letters addressed to Tina Louisa dated June 11, and upon review of all documents pertaining to the above matter, Louisa and Partners, Inc., would like to present the offer described herewith as settlement sum for the above-referenced matter. Said offer is for settlement purposes only and does not constitute an admission of liability.

Professional: After reviewing your 93A demand letter to Tina Louisa, dated June 11, and all the material pertaining to this matter, Louisa and Partners, Inc., would like to offer the following settlement. This offer is for settlement purposes only and in no way suggests that the company is at fault.

An insurance information sheet

Jargon: Paying for medical care is an example of the direct costs normally associated with workplace accidents. This cost can diminish if the employer utilizes our provider network and one of our personal providers renders the necessary services. In addition, there are indirect costs that must be considered. These include expenses for training and lost productivity, which equal and/or exceed medical care costs.

Professional: Workplace accidents directly impact employers since they must cover the cost of their employees' medical treatment. Of course, these expenses lessen when employees use doctors and other health professionals from our network. In addition, employers pay an equal or even greater price for training and lost productivity.

A manufacturing letter

Jargon: Stress analysis was performed again to determine the load necessary to fail the part considering the reduction in size of the newer model. The determination was inconclusive. Therefore, it is suggested that the part be disassembled, cleaned, and examined. After completion of this test, it should be observed in its operational state under normal conditions.

Relaxed: We performed a stress test to determine how much weight would cause the part to fail considering that the newer model was smaller than the older one. The test was inconclusive. As a next step, we would like to disassemble, clean, and examine the part, then observe it operating under normal conditions.

A consultant's report

Jargon: Solutions have been found for Dorman Oil to capture and leverage critical knowledge contained in manuals, reports, training materials, and in the human memory banks of the individual and collective employees. One of the above solutions is to refine isolated information and integrate it into the employee bank through multimedia and other technologies.

Relaxed: We have found solutions for Dorman Oil so it can benefit from the information within the company, including manuals, reports, training materials, and, of course, employees' know-how. One solution is for Dorman Oil to summarize key points in employee training sessions that incorporate multimedia and other technologies.

Take the risk!

I recently met with an editorial board of a large HMO. The problem: public image. The solution: lively, more reader-focused communications. During the meeting, I recommended several changes. One was that their writers eliminate industry jargon that transformed an everyday message into a threat.

You Have Now Entered
the Twilight Zone of Wordsmithing

Ah, how easily you pick up the newspaper or comb through a magazine enjoying the articles. And that coworker—the one with the desk beside yours—you read through his letters, make a few comments, say the writing's okay, and hand it back. Ah, the written word. That pleasant. That easy.

Once you start editing your own work, though, you get a strange, almost Twilight Zonesque insight into word use. First, you notice that awkward paragraph, wordy sentence, or jargon each time you write. You're annoyed, but nonchalant. After all, you can correct the problems and improve your skills with a little practice.

Suddenly you notice—your coworker, the one whose writing you see virtually every day—his writing is as wordy as yours, no actually, *more* wordy than yours. And that structure slips and slides like a first-time in-line skater. Why hadn't you noticed it before?

The situation escalates as you pick up your favorite newspaper and stare at the headline. Is there no rest? No peace from your new knowledge? You see how the paper ruthlessly twisted words to manipulate the readers' attention. And those passives; those sloppy sentences. And that condescending tone as if you, dear reader, would accept a K-Mart brand of wordsmithing rather than Macy's.

But don't worry! Your newfound knowledge needn't put you in readers' hell. It will highlight good writing in neon shades, giving you a spy's insight into messages that manipulate and helping you create better business documents. And that coworker—you can help him, too.

At that point, one of the vice presidents turned red and said, "We've been using that language for the full 20 years I've been with this company! Why should we change it now?" The answer was clear: *because* they had been using it for 20 years. Yet that vice president, along with so many others in the business world, was afraid of change. Fortunately, others in the meeting disagreed. As a focus group later revealed, the more relaxed tone won the readers' interest.

To upgrade your writing, take risks. Venture from the old and familiar into new and more challenging alternatives. The sentence doesn't sound right? Rewrite it. Don't like the tone? Tighten. But mostly, recognize that writing is the world's fastest-changing fashion. And you, the successful businessperson, must keep up with the changes.

TROUBLESHOOTING

You Say Active and She Says Passive—Facing the Boss

You write. Carefully, yet quickly. You check for problem 1: passives. Nope, nothing. You got them all. Then, problem 2: wordiness. Nope, you cut every extra article and preposition. Pleased, you show your boss, ready for her okay. Yet she hands back the paper with loops and letters from first line to last. You look closely and, surprised and disgusted, notice that she's inserted extra words and has replaced the active voice with the passive. What do you do? Depending on your boss, you make one of these two choices:

1. Explain the difference between the passive and active voice and wordy and concise word use as objectively as possible. Show her sections from this book as backup. Let her know that style is more a matter of contemporary mind-set and rules than of personal taste.

2. Ask whether what your boss says, goes. If so, keep the changes. It's unfair, but at least you have the satisfaction of knowing what's right when writing, what isn't, and why.

CONCLUSION

At this stage of rewriting, you should be ruthless about weeding out the passive voice, flat language, negativity, and all the other common problems of business writing. Learn to recognize them. Identify the problems that plague you most. Then skim through your document for their telltale signs.

Showing

Object: *To receive invaluable feedback within your time constraints for the most professional copy possible and for long-term improvement of your writing.*

Showing your writing to other people is perhaps the most underrated aspect of the writing process. You probably pass your writing around, asking coworkers or friends how it sounds. Your readers peruse the pages and hand back the document. "Good," they say. Or, "It's okay but I don't know what you mean in that third line there." You thank them, make a few changes, and send off the document.

This approach has one benefit: self-satisfaction. After all, another person likes your writing, so it must be good. So what if that person is as looped into your industry's tangle of jargon and tired word use as you are? So what if that person isn't an editor? And so what if that person doesn't know a passive from a misplaced modifier, or a colon from a comma?

A better idea: get solid, objective feedback that can provide a cornucopia of information to help you improve your document and gain critical insights into your writing skill. Without it, your writing becomes anemic and dry, withering like last summer's fruit.

Given the harried pace of your work life, try to receive feedback at two times.

1. *After you've finished editing your document*

Most likely you write and rewrite your letter in record speed, then rush to fling it in the fax machine or mailbox or zap it through the E-mail wires. Still, you do have time to show your document. Consider this scenario.

Scene: You're heading for the home stretch with your letter. The phone's ringing, two of your associates have signaled that they must talk, and you have another letter to write. You check your watch. The mail pickup is in 30 minutes. Yet you still aren't secure about this letter. It's an apology to an important client. What should you do?

At this point, give your letter to an associate who can quickly correct content or style problems. Either input the changes yourself, or have your editor make corrections directly on the computer. The document that ultimately reaches the client's desk will be markedly better.

Don't stop here. Save both the original and the edited versions and compare them later. This will give you insight into your writing strengths and weaknesses so that you need less editing help the next time around.

At times, you can leisurely assemble your document, writing and rewriting it one day and showing it the next. Be sure you get the most from your feedback, as in this scenario.

Scene: On the airplane home, you wrote a short report discussing the conference you just attended. You get to work the next day and read what you've written. It seems okay, but you want a second opinion. After all, this report might determine whether the company sends employees to the conference next year. You notice a coworker sitting at her desk flipping through some papers. She's a pretty good writer and doesn't look too busy. You ask her for feedback.

Rather than have her mark up the paper or tell you what changes to make, have her discuss the writing problems with you. Perhaps some of her corrections are subjective—she just happens to like one style better than another. Ultimately, you should decide. Perhaps some of her edits are rooted in writing principles. Write these down so you'll remember them next time. Finally, some of her suggestions may be based on the company's style. If so, determine whether these are your organization's bad habits or savvy decisions about correct wording.

2. After you've written and sent numerous documents

The all-at-once method is an extremely helpful way to receive valuable feedback. Show several of your documents to a coworker, friend, or other editor. This approach is especially useful when you can't receive feedback immediately after you've written your document:

Scene: You recently finished a proposal. Because of the deadline, your manager made changes and sent the copy to your potential customer. You didn't discuss why he made those changes; you didn't even see the finished copy. Actually, for the past month or two, you've written numerous letters and reports and haven't received feedback about any of them.

You call a friend from the communications department to ask if he has a half hour to review your writing. "Not this afternoon," your friend says, explaining that he has a tight deadline. "How about Friday? Around 3:00?" You make a date. When you get together, you get an overview of your good and bad habits and make a note to meet with your friend in a month or two for another review.

A Quick Look into the Writing Rumor Mill

There are more writing rumors than tabloid sightings of Elvis. Here are some of them.

The reader is always right

Somehow, a rumor got circulated in the business community and it prevails today—another person's opinion is always right. Thus, well-meaning businesspeople cut great opening lines, add tired expressions to otherwise lively writing, and imitate styles that went out decades ago just because someone told them to.

Another, more insidious, problem is that the unknowing reader may drop a line such as, "I guess writing isn't your forte," or "Maybe you should look into a writing class." Rather than being constructive, the comment hits your ego like a wrecker's ball, and for the next four weeks you're debilitated, word-use wise. At times like these remember, the reader is not always right.

The reader is usually wrong

This opinion sprouts from two seeds and gets cultivated in the competitive workplace. The first seed is defensiveness. How can a coworker know how to write better than you? And professional writers and editors? They don't understand your point. Their suggestions might make sense for some people, but not for you. The other seed is the old decide-for-yourself attitude. Don't like a comment? Forget it. Don't think an opinion's on target? Then it isn't. Throwing away good comments is like throwing away dollar bills. Don't do it.

This rumor contains smudges of truth. When you get a comment, be skeptical, especially when it comes from a coworker. Determine the logic behind the comment, too. Is the opinion based on taste? Forget it. If possible, show the document to two people. Find similiar comments? If so, they're probably valid.

Some people will never be good writers
no matter how much help they get

It's true, some people will never be good writers. In fact, most people will never be good writers if by good writers you mean such authors as William Faulkner, Alice Walker, or William Safire. On the other hand, almost everyone can cultivate the skills critical to writing basic business documents. People who can't may have a learning disability that affects their skill and can see a specialist who can reveal different routes to writing well.

I've Gotta Be Me!

In businesses everywhere you can hear the sad lament that bosses or coworkers edit out the writer's voice in favor of a more generic one. Writers are perplexed. After all, their names are at the bottoms of these letters. Their initials on those memos. Why can't they write in their own voices?

The answer is simple. Because at the top of the fax, memo, or letter page is another, more important, name—the company's. And you, the business writer, ultimately don't represent yourself even if you're writing a sales letter to someone you spoke to for hours. Wise companies understand the importance of a single, unified voice and work to make every correspondence consistent.

WANTED: EDITOR—THE RIGHT EDITOR

When seeking an editor, find someone who is a good writer, understands the content of your message, and is positive and encouraging. You will find editors in various facets of your life. Here are a few candidates with the pros and cons of each.

Friends

You're probably not about to invite a few friends over for a beer and a writing critique. But you may have a friend at work or one who is particularly good at writing who may volunteer feedback now and then. Most likely, you'll approach this person when you have an especially demanding project, such as a pressing proposal you bring home for the weekend or a brochure for your start-up business.

The best and the worst aspects of having friends edit your work are the same: they like you. The upside is they won't slander you or bruise your ego. Their comments will be largely positive; even the negative ones will be carefully and discreetly worded. The downside is that they may hedge a bit, avoiding telling you that a piece doesn't work.

Significant others

Significant others, or SO's as they're commonly called, tend to excel in the honesty arena—sometimes they excel too much. Sure, your SO may provide some very candid and helpful information, but you may feel like sleeping in a separate bed for a week or so.

The problem involves more than your feelings; it involves your SO's feelings, too. Say, for instance, that your significant other recommends you rewrite a press release because the message about your new product wouldn't interest even your mother. But you like the press release, and you'll implement a few of the suggested changes, but you won't implement them all. This could cause trouble when you bring the final rewrite home the next night. After all, you *did* ask your SO's advice. And your SO *did* spend quite a lot of time reading your press release and developing comments.

So, how can you get useful feedback from your significant other, aside from signing up for couples' counseling classes? First, make an agreement that you'll listen to your partner's comments, consider and value them, but only use the ones that make most sense to you. You, meanwhile, won't interrupt, grow defensive, or mention those comments later when, for example, you're fighting. Your significant other must agree to provide comments in the most open and positive way possible.

Coworkers

They sit two cubicles down the hall or two floors up. They understand the material you're writing about and will know when you've misrepresented it, since they write similar documents for similar audiences every week. They probably know or share your boss. And certainly they're sympathetic, especially when you go rushing by their desks throwing down that troublesome letter or report with a quick plea to please, please help.

On the other hand, coworkers can also be competitors. After all, companies have fewer positions the higher up you go, and you might compete for one of them. Your business may even foster competition. Such a relationship will certainly stymie a positive editorial association. In addition, coworkers may be as caught up in the company jargon as you are. Their suggestions and alternatives might just drag your writing deep into the muck of tired language.

The best suggestion when searching for a coworker-editor: choose carefully. You're hunting for sweet Concord grapes, not lemons.

Bosses

The boss—the most difficult and sometimes impossible kind of editor. The most common type of feedback from bosses is the unasked-for variety: whatever changes your boss wants, you make. Also, with your boss as editor you must face the old let's-not-discuss-this, let's-get-it-out, and we've-always-written-it-this-way approaches.

A boss as editor can be anxiety provoking. Your boss is the one who writes your evaluations, recommends you for promotions and raises, and shapes your future. Show the boss a weak letter or send a confusing report, and you don't get mere feedback. You get a black mark next to your name that may show up in your next evaluation.

Finally—and perhaps this is the biggest problem of all—bosses think they can write simply because they're bosses. Your boss makes more money than you do, right? And your boss has had more lunches with the president than you have, right? Perhaps your boss *is* the president. The fact that someone is your boss or can afford two houses while you have only one says nothing about that person's writing ability. Except, of course, that you must give in.

Having a boss as editor has pluses, too. For one, your boss certainly understands the product, service, or situation you're discussing and can give useful advice. Your boss can anticipate subtle but real problems your writing may create—whether a false promise that could cause legal problems or a tone that could stir customer wrath.

In addition, your boss has a stake in your success. What makes you look good, makes him or her look good, too. Finally, your boss has probably reviewed many documents like yours and may have a stronger sense of what works and what doesn't. Take notes. By understanding what your boss wants, you'll save yourself revision time later.

In-house writers and editors

If your organization has professional writers and editors, they probably can provide invaluable feedback rooted in basic writing principles and wrapped in objective language. However, there is a downside to professional writers as editors. They may be incredibly busy, scrambling harder than anyone else to make deadlines, perfect copy, and please anywhere from two to twenty people with one draft alone. A second, surprising consideration is that even professional writers may have serious writing problems, making their advice more offbeat than anyone else's.

Teachers

Okay, you're ready to enter the big leagues of feedback—writing classes. If you live near a large city—or even in some towns—you have two choices:

1. Classes at adult-education centers, churches, high schools, or even private living rooms. These classes are usually inexpensive and small enough so you get plenty of feedback. Teachers range from exceptional, seasoned professionals who teach for the love of teaching, to novices who need a few extra bucks, to small business owners trying to drum up business. Participants tend to be a mixture of high school grads opting for self-improvement, businesspeople trying to upgrade their skills, bored retirees looking for entertainment, and single people searching for dates.

2. Evening college courses. Teachers of evening classes are frequently professors by day as well, although an occasional rookie will slip in undaunted by the weird hours or low pay. Participants are a blend of ages and backgrounds, although

class makeup tends to be a bit more homogeneous than in the adult education counterparts. On the downside, college evening classes cost a bundle.

Whichever option you choose, take advantage of your teacher. Ask if you can show some of your at-work material. Always write down your teacher's most consistent comments and return to those each time you edit yourself.

Receiving a Harmonious Edit

Imagine listening to a symphony orchestra playing Beethoven. You love how the flutes carry the melody, appreciate the violins' soft wail, are moved by the percussion's booming crescendos. But unless you're an experienced musician, you certainly couldn't explain the technicalities of the music nor would you notice nuances from one concert to the next. Writing is similar. Someone with only a remote understanding of language can give you only remote feedback. Someone unfamiliar with content can only vaguely explain whether your content is clear. When choosing an editor, chose an orchestra leader—an expert to help you create harmony from content and style. Ask your editor to

- *Provide objective feedback.* Make sure your editor provides you with comments based on sound principles and grammar rules, not on taste. Rather than an editor who says:

    This newsletter article is incredibly boring.

  find one who will say:

    Cut those tired phrases and your newsletter article will be more interesting.

  Make sure you have an editor who won't say:

    This bio is totally self-aggrandizing.

but says instead:

> This bio needs to focus on your experience, not on you.

Most readers won't know the right vocabulary. Your editor may want to explain that your report is plagued with repeated ideas, but may say only that it's slow. Your mission is to self-medicate. Once your reader has pointed out the symptom, you find the problem.

- *Discuss changes rather than make them.* Beware of the editor who reads your writing, then takes out a pen and starts making changes. Those changes might be based on taste—primarily the editor's. And even if the suggestions are great, you won't learn unless you know the rationale behind them. Your editor should ask for your opinions, why you chose certain words or decided to include or omit information.

- *Be forward looking.* Editing is a process of making a document better, not pointing out why it's bad. Make sure your editor helps you see advantages, not mistakes. For example, you don't want an editor who'll say:

> The structure of your report is completely illogical; no one could possibly follow what you're trying to say.

but one who will take this approach:

> This piece needs a more logical structure. Try a tight chronological order to connect each event.

Your editor should remind you of the positive sides of your writing. Rather than saying:

> This information sheet is snobby and boring. No one will read it.

your editor should say:

> This information sheet contains a lot of important information. Great. Now make the tone more friendly.

- *Be respectful.* Most professional writers have met editors who laughed at their writing, suggested they find work flipping hamburgers at McDonald's, or told them to rewrite from scratch a piece they'd worked on for months. Professional writer, CEO, or secretary—insults help no one. So if your editor jokes about your style, teases you about your spelling, or laughs at your letters, you have two choices: (1) politely ask your editor to stop making negative comments, or (2) refuse to show that person your work again.

- *Maintain confidentiality.* Like most people, you are probably sensitive about your writing ability. So make sure your editor will keep every aspect of your discussion confidential, from content to writing style. The exception is when managers or coaches review your work and then include their impressions in an evaluation. In this case, treat the write-up as yet another learning experience informing you of strong and problem areas.

TRY THIS! Find someone in your organization who is writing documents similar to yours but has different habits—good and bad. Then arrange a schedule for editing each other, perhaps once a week or, if you have considerable material, once a day. Learn from each other's mistakes and note each other's accomplishments. A good tip here: always start with praise so you don't blush from criticism.

The Truth about Training

Writing seminars. Almost every organization has them or has had them at one time. Employees shuffle into the training room for a three- to six-hour session featuring an array of information. They take notes, work on handouts, are surprised and a little frightened by all they do not know. When the seminar is over, they fill out evaluation forms letting the higher-ups know whether they liked the class and the teacher and whether they'd apply all they learned to their documents later.

In the end, the company executives feel good because they've invested in upgrading their employees' skills and, in the process, their corporate voice; the participants feel good because they learned something; and the trainers feel good because everyone loved their classes. If the trainers are consultants, they're especially happy because they made good money and have another client name to put in their information packets.

The one glitch to this glee is that participants generally forget 97 percent of what they learned within two weeks. The reason: One seminar can't possible break a lifetime of bad habits. Nor can it revitalize the company voice that fosters those habits. By the month's end, most organizations are left with a residue of good feelings, a few handouts, and nothing else.

If you do attend these seminars, be sure to take scrupulous notes. Bring some of your own writing, too. As the class reviews one writing problem after another, check your own documents. If you find that problem, add it to your rewriting list.

READING IT RIGHT

Feedback comes in three distinct styles.

Line by line

When to use: When you have enough time to review and input the suggested changes.

Benefits: You have more control over the edits, improve the document, and break your bad habits by correcting the problems line by line.

Drawbacks: Inputting the changes takes time.

This popular type of editing evolved from the old days of teachers' comments that landed in inky stains across paragraphs or even

Editing Marks

Editing marks can save a lot of time and space—if you and your editor agree on what they mean. Otherwise, you might as well ask a two-year-old to scribble all over your technical report. Here are the most commonly used editing marks. Share this page with your editor.

Take out	Words at at Work
Insert	Words Work
Transpose	Work at Words
Close up	Word s at Work
Add space	Words at Work
Make lowercase	Words At Work
Make uppercase	Words at work
Underline or italicize	Words at Work
Don't underline or italicize	*Words at Work*
Boldface	Words at Work
Start new paragraph	Words at Work This method of improving your business writing will save you time, toil, and money.
Make lines line up	Words at Work
	This method of improving your business writing will save you time, toil, and money.
Ignore handwritten change	Words at Work

pages, in remarks in the margins and questions scrawled between lines. Some editors draw little frowning faces at particularly difficult passages. The benefits of this kind of editing are many. For starters, you can see your original writing and the corrections at one time. This gives you the opportunity to compare in a quick before-and-after fashion.

In addition, this editing style usually contains explanations for the changes. At times, the comments can be cruel, with little "huh's?" in the margins and lines such as "This doesn't make any sense," and "Do you really expect the reader to know what you're talking about here?" At other times, of course, they can be encouraging and constructive.

Here is a sample edit of a newsletter article:

> ~~It was announced by the company today~~ that the human resources department ~~will be welcoming~~ a new Vice President ~~whose name is Shelia Abbot.~~ ~~In the past,~~ Miss Abbot worked in the Human Resources Department ~~at~~ Maxwell Company. ~~She also worked in the Human Resources Department~~ Thompson & Chardes. Shelia said she ~~is~~ thrilled to be ~~in~~ as dynamic and exciting a company as ours. ~~She attended~~ Radcliff College ~~as an undergraduate and~~ received a master's ~~in sociology from~~ Ohio State. ~~She will join us on January 3.~~

Handwritten edits: Today, · Sheila Abbot · joining · starting January 3 · s of · at · and · was · A graduate of · e · where she · degree

Rewrites

When to use: When you don't have time to input changes and your editor is a better writer than you are.

Benefits: A better piece at no time cost to you.

Drawbacks: Even if you read the revision, your skill won't improve significantly.

Frequently, rewrites seem ideal. You simply hand your document over to someone else; that person reads, types a little of this and that, and—instant improvement. Meanwhile, you can be writing another letter, getting a cup of coffee, or doing virtually anything else that interests you.

In terms of improving your writing style, however, rewrites are a little like hiring a personal trainer to help you exercise, then snuggling up on a couch and watching the trainer work out. You simply cannot improve your style by rereading someone's edits of your work. On the other hand, your schedule might be sealed tighter than a peanut in a shell. In this case, go ahead and ask for a rewrite. Just make sure that your editor is

- a good writer
- familiar with the content
- flexible enough to complete the rewrite by your deadline

Here's a rewritten version of the paragraph from the line-by-line section:

> Today, the company announced that Sheila Abbot will be joining the Human Resources Department as Vice President starting January 3. A graduate of Radcliffe College and Ohio State, where she received a master's degree, Ms. Abbot worked in the Human Resources Departments of Maxwell Company and Thompson & Chardes. Sheila said she was thrilled to be in as dynamic and exciting a company as ours.

Critiques

When to use: When you haven't had feedback for months or more and have at least four or five finished documents.

Benefits: Better insights into your overall habits.

Drawbacks: You won't have the opportunity to implement changes.

Here's the big one—a critique that sweeps through your document like a gardener's hoe, turning up your good habits and bad.

PIT STOP

Ouch! Getting feedback about your writing can be as pleasant as poking your finger into a food grinder. Perhaps Bobby McFerrin's lyric, "Don't worry, be happy," may be overstating it a bit, but the idea is basically on target. When you receive comments, don't worry about hidden implications, such as, say, that you're not a good writer. Don't feel embarrassed, or dig up reasons to defend your writing, either. Put your ego in a box and leave it there until you've heard every comment.

Your job seems simple, at first. Read through the suggestions, grasp the ideas, and learn. But learning passively is never enough. You must apply the suggestions and return to them each time you write until you break your bad habits. Also, be sure to remember these critique dos and don'ts:

Don't read your critiques to determine whether you are a good or bad writer.

Do look for individual problems you can realistically address.

Don't view suggestions as judgments.

Do see weaknesses as mechanical problems, which, with consistent and focused tweaking, you can fix.

Don't simply put the critique away once you finish reading it.

Do make a list of your bad habits from most to least prevalent and edit according to those.

Don't accept unsubstantiated opinions.

TRY THIS! In a file, either paper or electronic, save all your first drafts for at least a month and monitor your growth. Try again a month or two later. Perhaps review your findings with your editor. You may feel comfortable with your growth, or you may want to chart a course so you can improve even faster.

PIT STOP

Read these reminders before and/or after showing your writing:

- Writing strong business documents does not require a superior intellect, Harvard education, or genetic ability reserved for journalists at the *Washington Post*. Rather, it requires knowing the mechanics of language, much as assembling lawn furniture requires knowing which bolt fits in which hole. It's that simple.

- Treat criticism as a gift. If you don't like it, don't use it. But be polite and say thank you.

- Your editor isn't an enemy, insulting you and gloating behind your back. This person, whether a business associate or spouse, is exerting energy to help you improve.

- Repeat these words—"I *can* write well, I *can* write well, I *can* write well"—no matter how intense or confusing the feedback you receive.

Do ask for examples that will both support and illustrate the comment.

Don't focus most of your attention on negative comments.

Do recognize that positive comments are as valid as negative ones.

Here is an example of a good editor's critique:

> Your writing contains enough specific information to make the message interesting and believable. It would be stronger, though, if you cut extra words. In the article about Sheila Abbot, for example, you write: "It was announced by the company today that the human resources department will be welcoming a new Vice President whose name is Sheila Abbot." Your shorter, more interesting message would read: "Today, the company announced that Sheila Abbot will join the Human Resources Department as Vice President."

TROUBLESHOOTING

The Content Move-Around

You ask for feedback. Or maybe you don't ask, but you get it. And the majority of changes relate to content, more time-consuming and frustrating than an all-red jigsaw puzzle. The solution is to show your original list to your editor. Get feedback, play with the order together, settle any content problems up front. Then, if necessary, show your editor the draft before you edit for structure.

This Feedback Would Make Perfect Sense . . . If Only I Understood It!

You get feedback written on the margins on your page or typed on a separate piece of paper. Your editor—a coworker renowned for his

---

One Hundred Frenchmen, and Other Aspects of the Resiliency Test

You're not sure what happened. But, suddenly, you're writing a proposal for what could be the biggest account in the company's history. Millions of dollars hover between your moist fingertips and the keys you punch to articulate a message. Finally, you finish, edit for structure . . . fine, word use . . . change those general expressions into specific ones. Then you show not one, but two of your coworkers. You flip the pages, read their comments. Now you're ready to make changes. Except for one problem. Your editors commented on everything from the way you presented key benefits to your comma use.

What do you do? Give your editors' comments the resiliency test. First, see how well their comments stand up against logic. If, for example, one editor suggests that you heap in jargon for a more professional and credible message, don't. Why add dull words and phrases when you're striving to create interest? Next, see whether your editors' comments are consistent with each other and with comments you've received before. If they are, you'd better edit. For as the old adage says, "If one hundred Frenchmen say you're drunk, you'd better go sit down."

---

skills. Or maybe a boss with a perfect understanding of the material. You know this person's advice must be helpful, except there's one problem: you don't understand any of it. The solution is easy. Simply arrange to discuss the edits. In-person discussions are best, since you can look at the copy together, flip to other sections, pull out support documents and read through them together. If meeting in person isn't possible, try the telephone.

CONCLUSION

Never be shy about showing your unfinished document to someone you trust. After all, quality matters most in a compelling message. Make sure your editor understands how to edit. Make sure you listen to his or her suggestions. And in the end, trust your own judgment.

Proofreading

Object: *To immediately identify problem punctuation, spelling, and other usage issues for a uniquely professional document.*

Great. You've done it! Ripped through that document in record time, listing, writing, rewriting, and, yes, even showing your message. You think you're finished. Actually, you're sure you're finished. Wait! One more step left. And yes, you absolutely must take it, whether you've spell checked, grammar checked, or anything-else checked your writing. That step: proofreading. Let's start by looking at the basics.

Print out before proofing. This little act, as simple as pressing "ctrl" and "p," makes the difference between sight and blindness when proofing. Why? Who can say? Perhaps because you see the full page instead of one section at a time. Or maybe because you get a new perspective with hard copy. Or maybe the copy's easier to read. Proofing on paper is much like exercise. You don't know exactly why it's so good for you, but it is.

Check for bad habits. Treat usage problems like word-use problems: find your bad habits and correct them. Where do you turn in the blizzard of usage rules? On a scale of 1 to 10, with 10 at the top:

- Feedback from knowledgeable individuals: 10
- Grammar-check programs and updated handbooks: 5

- Old handbooks: 1
- Old sayings: −1

Let someone else take a second look when possible. You've looked at your writing and looked and looked until it's a smear of indistinguishable symbols. That's why having someone else proof your writing is so important. You'll be amazed—and possibly embarrassed—to notice the little faux pas that scream out to even a semi-literate reader.

TRY THIS! Go to your desk or briefcase and find some letters you've recently written. Then, check for each of the points listed in the following section of this chapter. To get the clearest idea of your writing habits, look at three or four letters, not just one. Keep a list of your most common foibles and check for them the next time you write a letter.

The World's Easiest Edit—Guaranteed!

The first part of proofing is as simple as creating white space. In fact, it is creating white space, giving shape and definition to your message. Think for a moment of how you respond when you are reading a book or magazine and one paragraph runs for half the page. You probably skim the page wearily, flick ahead to see how much more you must read, or put the article away.

That's why newspapers and magazines—from *People* to *Newsweek*—keep their articles short, loading the page with sidebars and photographs to break the monotony of black ink on white paper. To compete, your writing must proclaim itself boldly from the page.

To start, look at your document. If a mass of black ink has landed on the page, start breaking up that paragraph. Where do you break? Between thoughts? Probably not, or your paragraph will run like the Mississippi. Better break at transitions between times, for example, or between statement and support.

Beware of Two-Sided Rules

Determine which of these sentences is correct:

> First, we should arrange a conference call in my office.

or

> First we should arrange a conference call in my office.

Answer: Both.

Now, determine which of these is correct:

> Either I'll call you or you'll call me Tuesday morning.

or

> Either I will contact you or you will contact me Tuesday morning.

Answer: Again, both.

The English language is loaded with choices, adding new meaning to the old saying that rules are made to be broken. The only rule you can't break, regardless of mood and circumstance, is consistency. If you call someone Ms. Smith at the start of a document, don't call her Miss Smith later. If you use contractions, as in "You're really interesting," don't say, "You are really interesting" later (unless you mean to emphasize the word *are*, as in "People say otherwise, but you *are* interesting."). Variety is great for a wardrobe, but in this case, it creates disaster.

Next, look at your font. Make sure the lettering is clear and large enough to attract a reader. Times New Roman is great, but **City Medium** bombs. Also, make sure you distinguish your headings.

Finally, you don't want your writing to float on a paper lake, surrounded by white space. For this reason, make sure you

- have at least two lines per paragraph
- bullet phrases, sentences, or even paragraphs, but not words
- center your message on the page
- avoid second letter pages with only a few lines at the top

Once your document has the right look, give it polish by checking for those little, important details that are as distracting to your readers as ink on a white suit jacket. Now, compare these examples:

Jackson Consulting, Inc., E-mail Guidelines

Many employees are now sending electronic mail to customers and fellow workers.

Always be sure your all your correspondence is:

- Professional. You need to uphold the company's image in electronic messages as well as letters through the mail. Therefore, be sure you use professional language.

- Discreet. External clients—and competitors—can have access to your message, so never discuss sensitive company issues.

- Business-related. Use E-mail for messages pertaining to the business only. That means send no messages home and no chatty hellos to fellow employees electronically.

Jackson Consulting, Inc., E-mail Guidelines

When sending E-mail to customers and fellow workers, always be sure all your correspondence is:

- *Professional.* You need to uphold the company's image in electronic messages as well as letters through the mail. Therefore, be sure you use professional language.

- *Discreet.* External clients—and competitors—can have access to your message, so never discuss sensitive company issues.

- *Business-related.* Use E-mail for messages pertaining to the business only. That means send no messages home and no chatty hellos to fellow employees electronically.

LETTERS: THE ULTIMATE CHECKLIST

No business communication is as loaded with details to remember as the letter. The following checklist spotlights the essentials for brilliant, reader-ready letters:

Writer's address—Usually on letterhead or in left corner of paper:

> Bancroft Paper Company
> 43 Green Street
> Providence, RI 02903-3279

Dateline: June 1, 1997

Reader's address: Bob George
                   32 Millers Lane
                   Everytown, RI 02124

Salutation: Dear Bob,

Introduction: You now have the opportunity to join thousands of Rhode Island business executives who have selected Bancroft Paper Company for all their envelopes, stationery, inserts, and other paper products. And, with our Paper Plan, you can choose from the largest selection of paper in the state. You'll also receive a special identification number that entitles you to free delivery any time—day or night.

Body: But that's not all. Our Paper Plan entitles you to valuable discounts on graphic design services from leading designers throughout the state, and consultations on the right look for everything from newsletters to brochures. You'll also receive *Graphics Times*, an exclusive quarterly newspaper featuring articles of special interest to our customers. Want to know what's new in direct mail pieces or holiday stuffers? Then attend the annual Products

	Convention at the City Trade Center at a 25% discount just by mentioning Bancroft Paper Company's name.
Closing:	I am sending along some paper samples as well as our competitive price sheet. If you have any questions, please call. Otherwise, I'll call next week.
Complimentary closing:	Sincerely,
Signature block:	Gemma Lymn Sales Representative
	Enclosures (3)

Paragraph style

Make sure your letters are in the full block style with everything—date, salutation, closing, and body—flush left. This gives your letters a clean, streamlined look and is easy to create since you don't have to bother indenting. Your computer should determine the number of spaces between paragraphs and the width of your margins. If it does not, make your margins about 1¼ inch on the sides and bottom and about 2½ inches on the top.

ONE-PARAGRAPH PHOBIA

I don't know why, exactly, but most businesspeople mistakenly believe that one-paragraph letters are taboo. So they tack one-liners at the top of the letter, then add another sentence or two to the body, making the letter look more like a list than a narrative. Actually, one-paragraph letters are fine, even desirable when appropriate. They make a strong, direct point, which the reader can absorb in one verbal mouthful.

Check: Whether your letter has a well-defined border, like a frame around a picture.

Writer's address

Most likely, you're using stationery with your company's name, address, and telephone number printed on the page, so don't bother adding your address. Some people like to handwrite their name somewhere at the top of the page. Nice touch, but not necessary. Your name will be at the bottom of the letter—why write it twice?

If you're not writing on company stationery, type your name, company name, and address in the upper left, three spaces above the date.

Check: Typos in your address. Nothing is as embarrassing as misspelling your own name or street address.

Date line

The date line is exactly what it says, the line for the date. Americans write: June 15, 1996. Europeans write: 15 June 1996

Lots of people think they should use the European date when writing to an international audience. But that's a bit pretentious and highly inconsistent, since you're using American spelling for all other words.

Which date is right if you're sending a letter on the 15th but wrote it on the 14th? The 14th. The date line says when you wrote your message; the postmark says when you mailed it.

Check: The correct date.

Reader's address

When you write the reader's name, title, company name, and address, you have the dubious opportunity to insult your reader via misspellings. Stay safe:

- Spell the person's name correctly. People tend to be touchy about this, as if misspelling a name means you don't like it. Check common names that have uncommon variations, such as Smith or

Smyth and Lesley or Leslie. Be doubly careful with businesses that ignore usage rules in favor of creativity in names, from ValuFlex to DISCO.

- Use Ms. or Mr. appropriately. This is a tough one, too, when you're writing to women. The new business-writing norm is to call all women "Ms." unless they indicate their preference for "Miss" or "Mrs." However, insult is a pretty big room, and people find reasons to enter. They may be insulted by "Ms." simply because they're not used to it or by "Mrs." because their marital status shouldn't matter.

Another area of sensitivity is gender. Say you get a call from Sandy Morris, Lee Smith, Lesley Jacobson, or Andy Crowley. Determining the caller's gender is much like flipping a coin. Keep the change in your pocket, though, and choose one of these options:

1. Write out the person's full name:

   Dear Lesley Jacobson,

2. Call the company or person and find out. If you're lucky, you'll get a secretary who will understandingly tip you off. Be sure to ask, "How does Lesley Jacobson like to be addressed?" and not, "Is Lesley a guy?"

Finally, be careful of professional titles, using them only when appropriate. Some people, such as Ph.D.'s who call themselves "Dr.," love titles. Others don't. I've been a bona fide professor, but "Professor Benjamin" was too stuffy for my taste. Once again, the best way to determine whether a title is appropriate is to find out your readers' preference. If you can't find out, you'll have to guess.

- Include the correct job title after the person's name. If the title is especially long (for example, "Assistant Senior Manager of Internal and External Operations") break it into two lines and indent the second line two spaces. But don't lop off a few words for convenience' sake or guess at a title.

What's in a Name? Better Find Out

One of the few rules for business products, services, and newsletter titles is to break rules. So, when writing to or about a company—even your own—check to make sure you have the correct

Spelling: Particularly in the retail world, you find unusual, even startling, ways to spell otherwise basic words, such as "kidz" rather than "kids," "luv" instead of "love" and "valu" not "value."

Punctuation: Some organizations, particularly law firms, drop the commas between names; others add dashes between words; still others, rightly or wrongly, omit apostrophes. For example, "Cromley Smith and Andersen," "The National Manufacturers Organization," and "In-A-Second Temp Agency," could also be "Cromley, Smith and Andersen," "The National Manufacturers' Organization," and "In a Second Temp Agency."

Use of lower- and uppercase: Is the name "The Paper and Envelope Company" or "The Paper And Envelope Company" or the "Paper and Envelope Company" or the "Paper And Envelope" company? Only the company knows for sure.

Spacing: Companies get creative here, especially with newsletter names. For example, the correct spacing for one newsletter is: *UpwardDirections.* And for another, *NewsLink Today.*

Some organizations change their names as quickly as they hire and fire employees. This practice can be extreme. The president and founder of one of my clients—a successful operation with 600 employees—didn't know that the company's name contained "Group" and not "Company" as it had years before. So remember, before writing a company's name—and, in some cases, even your own company's name—check.

• Include the right street address, spelling out "Street," "Road," "Avenue," and so on, and numbers under 11:

  One Beacon Street
  13 Morningside Road

Remember, when writing the state, use the post office's two-letter abbreviations, such as RI for Rhode Island. Since most aren't that easy to figure out, here's a list of post office abbreviations for U.S. states, territories, and possessions:

Alabama	AL	Montana	MT
Alaska	AK	Nebraska	NE
American Samoa	AS	Nevada	NV
Arizona	AZ	New Hampshire	NH
Arkansas	AR	New Jersey	NJ
California	CA	New Mexico	NM
Canal Zone	CZ	New York	NY
Colorado	CO	North Carolina	NC
Connecticut	CT	North Dakota	ND
Delaware	DE	Northern Mariana Is.	CM
Dist. of Columbia	DC	Ohio	OH
Florida	FL	Oklahoma	OK
Georgia	GA	Oregon	OR
Guam	GU	Pennsylvania	PA
Hawaii	HI	Puerto Rico	PR
Idaho	ID	Rhode Island	RI
Illinois	IL	South Carolina	SC
Indiana	IN	South Dakota	SD
Iowa	IA	Tennessee	TN
Kansas	KS	Texas	TX
Kentucky	KY	Trust Territories	TT
Louisiana	LA	Utah	UT
Maine	ME	Vermont	VT
Maryland	MD	Virginia	VA
Massachusetts	MA	Virgin Islands	VI
Michigan	MI	Washington	WA
Minnesota	MN	West Virginia	WV
Mississippi	MS	Wisconsin	WI
Missouri	MO	Wyoming	WY

And here's a list of postal abbreviations for Canada:

Alberta	AB	Nova Scotia	NS
British Columbia	BC	Ontario	ON
Manitoba	MB	Prince Edward Island	PE
New Brunswick	NB	Quebec	PQ
Newfoundland	NF	Saskatchewan	SK

With overseas addresses, replicate whatever is on the stationery, such as this U.K. address:

Laurence Hartcliff
48, Sutcliffe Drive,
Leamington Spa,
Warwickshire,
CV33 XLD

A U.S. address might look something like this:

Ms. Elaine Jackson
Vice President, Human Resources
ValuFlex Corporation
Ten Roadway Avenue
Providence, RI 00021

The reader's address for an individual would look like this:

Mr. Richard Hold
12357 Village Green, Apt. #25
Belworth, MA 01602

Salutation

Since your main objective when writing a letter is to get the reader's attention fast, be sure to personalize your message whenever possible. Try to open your letter with a person's name. If you can't, then write "Dear Sir or Madam." "To whom it may concern" is as old and bland as Lawrence Welk reruns.

The next question is whether to use a colon, comma, or dash after the salutation. Generally, the colon is more formal and is appropriate for everything from daily business letters to invitations to, say, a $5,000-a-plate fund-raising dinner:

Dear Governor Winthrop:

However, the comma is less formal, more friendly, and a more personal way to greet your reader.

Check: Whether you've addressed the person consistently in both salutation and return address.

Introductory paragraph

Begin your first paragraph two lines below the salutation. Think space appeal here, and limit your opener to two to five lines. Beware of one-line paragraphs, which seem skimpy.

Check: Size and friendliness of the first line.

Body

Here's where most people collect words like freebies at a yard sale. Remember to make the body of your letter desirable by

- limiting each paragraph to 10 or 15 lines
- avoiding one-line paragraphs (they appear skimpy and tend to float on the page)
- separating your paragraphs with blank lines
- using bullets when you have numerous steps or points

Check: Size of paragraphs and the amount of information in each one.

Second page

According to one old saying, give readers a one-page letter and they may read that page; give readers a two-page letter and they will ignore both. But what if you have more information then will fit on a single page? The answer's easy: create enclosures, whether lists, paragraphs, or directions detailing new procedures.

If you just have to write a second page, type the reader's name on the top line, 1½ inches from the top, the date on the next line, and "page" and the page number one line below that, shown here:

Dr. Leonard Fuller
March 18, 1993
Page 2

Check: Whether you truly need that second page. If you do, just make sure you don't have a few words hanging on the top of the page or, even worse, that you don't devote an entire page to a signature block with a wash of white space beneath it.

Closing paragraph

Your closing paragraph is more than a good-bye. It's where you mention enclosures—whether articles, forms, or information sheets—and make future plans. Keep your paragraphs short and sweet:

> I have enclosed a brochure about our winter retreat. Please contact me if you have any questions.

Also, make sure your message is as proactive as possible. Rather than say:

> Call me if you are interested.

say:

> I'll call you next week unless I hear from you sooner.

Check: Whether you've included a specific date for your next contact.

Complimentary closing

Place your closing two lines below the end of the closing paragraph. Stick with the professional yet personal "Sincerely" unless you know the person well. Don't bother with "Very truly yours"—it's boring and old-fashioned. And avoid "Thanking you in advance," and other variations on the thank-you theme unless your reader has actually done something for you.

Check: Relax, complimentary closings are hard to overlook.

Signature block

At the end of your letter, leave three lines of blank space for your signature. Type your name and position beneath that if it's not on your letterhead. Then sign:

Sincerely,

Ann Marie Doherty
Human Resource Representative

Check: Oddly, plenty of people forget to sign their letters. So check.

Enclosure line and copies distributed

Let your reader know when you have enclosed materials by including an enclosure line two spaces beneath the typed signature in one
of these ways:

> Enclosure
> Enclosures (3)
> Encl.
> Encl. Financial reports
> Encl. 3 (pages)

The letter *c*, which stands for "copy," has replaced the "cc," or "car-
bon copy," of old. It follows the enclosure line and lets the reader
know of anyone else who received the letter. List the names in alpha-
betical order or by rank:

> c. Tom Burns
>   Lily Stanforde
>   Tina Rank
> c. Office of the President
>   Senior Manager's Office

Check: Correct use of enclosure and copy lines.

MEMO MAKEOVERS

With memos, check for many of the same problems you look for in
letters: correct spelling of your reader's name, correct date, interesting first line. The job is easier, though, since memos are basically

letters without the fuss and bother—no introductory paragraph, body, or closing. You don't even need a salutation or complimentary closing. Here's a brief memo checklist.

Headers

Headers are a quick-and-easy version of the salutation and signature block. At about 2¾ inches from the top of the page, type:

    TO:
    FROM:
    RE:
    DATE:

with a line between each.

Check: Whether your headers are in the right order. Also, since headers take the place of salutations and signature blocks, don't use "Sincerely" or other closings on your memo or fax sheet.

Body

As with letters, begin writing two lines below the date line. Don't bother making a connection to the reader or personalizing the memo. Just get out your message immediately.

Check: Whether your first few words are interesting and direct. As with letters, make sure your first paragraph—and all paragraphs— is a reasonable length.

Second page

Keep your memo to one page if at all possible. If you must use two pages, be sure the left, right, and bottom margins of the second page are the same as those of the first. At the top, however, create the following setup one inch down the page:

    MEMORANDUM
    October 1, 1993
    Page 2

Continue writing the memo four lines below the page number.

Make a Decision and Stay with It!

Although business writing is besieged with rules, you do have choices. In fact, you have lots of choices. And you should make them immediately or risk one of the greatest writing fumbles of all—inconsistency. For example, when writing about people in general, will you use "he and she," "s/he," or "they"? "They," in a sentence such as, "When a customer walks in the store, be sure they receive assistance within 30 seconds," is acceptable although "customer" is singular and "they" is plural. However, readers are likely to think this is a mistake. "S/he" sounds awkward. "He and she" is more common and probably the best option.

Here are some other choices:

Choice	Difference
Comma or dashes	Commas are more formal; dashes lighten the tone
Italic or underlining	Italic is a newer *and* more common form
Ms. or Miss/Mrs.	Ms. is more contemporary, although some readers prefer Miss or Mrs.
Dashes or colons	Colons are more formal and put a stop to the message; dashes usually slow down the message, more like commas
a.m. or AM	No real difference
Colon, dash, or comma after a salutation	A colon is formal, a dash informal, and a comma in between
Exclamation point or period	Exclamation points tell readers they should be excited; periods let the words do it
Times New Roman, Arial, or other fonts	Times New Roman is the most common; using alternative fonts depends on the document
Esquire or Attorney	Esquire is the older form; see what the lawyer wants to be called

Check: Whether you can avoid a second page. If not, set up the heading correctly.

Enclosures

Structure your enclosure notice as you would with letters:

> Enclosure
> Enclosures (3)
> Encl.
> Encl. Financial reports
> Encl. 3 (pages)

Distribution list for numerous readers

If you're including between three and ten readers, list their names at the bottom of the memo, beginning two lines below your last line. Type: "DISTRIBUTION:" then list the name and mail address of each reader. On each copy, highlight the recipient's name.

Check: Correct use of enclosure and distribution lines.

E-MAIL EDITING

Since electronic-mail messages are the newest form of written communication, no rigid conventions govern their use. And, you don't have to worry about format because you can't know how your message will look on your reader's screen. Still, review the following points before hitting the "Send" button.

Subject

Does your subject line headline your message in a concise way? Does it immediately say something interesting to your reader? Is it short enough (20 characters or so) not to get snipped in transmission? If you're sending to an E-mailbox shared by two or more people, use the subject line to state the name of your reader: "FOR BOBBI: sales figures."

Check: For an accurate and intriguing subject line.

Salutation

E-mail messages don't need a "Dear Prof. Walker" opening, but politeness is always a plus when you first write to someone. For shorter messages after you've established a relationship, you can drop the greeting.

Body

Since people write, read, and reply to E-mail quickly, misunderstandings can grow faster than dandelions on a spring lawn. For this reason, use short paragraphs and direct, factual sentences. Also, avoid "flaming," exchanging nasty messages, which is a part of the Internet's history. Instead, use the polite and professional tone appropriate for mailed or faxed communications.

Remember that the Internet transmits only standard typewriter characters. Long dashes, curly apostrophes and quotation marks, accent symbols, and other characters get scrubbed out, or changed into mysterious combinations—such as ^N—when they enter the Internet. Also, boldface and italic formatting disappears. To emphasize words or indicate the title of a book or other work, type *asterisks* or _underlines_ on either side of the phrase. Avoid typing in ALL CAPITAL LETTERS, which some people interpret as shouting.

Check: That your message is quick and easy to read.

Signature

A signature is unnecessary in most E-mail messages. But when writing to strangers, it's helpful to sign your message with your name, title, company, and E-mail address for replies. Don't succumb to the temptation to add cute artwork, clever quotations, or unnecessary disclaimers. Leave such personal expression for your personal messages.

Check: That a salutation and your signature appear in messages to people you haven't corresponded with before.

Reply

When you reply to someone else's E-mail message, some programs copy the original message on the bottom of the new one. If you can, edit that material so that it includes the parts of the message you're addressing. Be sure to include only relevant data.

Check: That you won't fill your reader's E-mailbox with unneeded data.

THE BUSINESS WORLD'S MOST SPECTACULAR USAGE PROBLEMS

Detecting usage problems is easy once you know what to target. To find your soft spots, read the following rules and determine which ones you consistently break. Take the quizzes, too. Get one wrong? Read the explanation so you know the rule and can correct the problem the next time you start to make it.

Abbreviations

Which is correct?

>   a. A researcher from our division gave a talk about computerized axial tomography (CAT) scans.
>
>   b. A researcher from our division gave a talk about CAT scans (computerized axial tomography scans).

Answer: a.

Why: The first time you mention a word that you plan to abbreviate, write it completely, placing the abbreviation in parentheses immediately afterwards. Capitalize all the abbreviated letters even if you wouldn't capitalize the actual name. Then use the abbreviation throughout the document.

Exceptions: Most abbreviations do not take periods, although some, such as "U.S.," "U.N.," and "U.K." do when you use them as adjectives with a noun immediately afterward: *The U.S. Treasury Department contacted us about a bid.*

Which is correct?

    a. Design Limited has sent us a proposal for a poster advertising our new children's toy.

    b. Design Ltd. has sent us a proposal for a poster advertising our new children's toy.

Answer: Both.

Why: Some standards do exist for business abbreviations—Company (Co.); Corporation (Corp.); Incorporated (Inc.); Limited (Ltd.)—but many companies create unique variations. Always investigate how a company spells its name, either by calling or by looking at its stationery.

Which is correct?

    a. Most of our customers live in southern California.

    b. Most of our customers live in southern CA.

Answer: a.

Why: When writing about a state, spell out the entire name.

Which is correct?

    a. We sent his bill to 654 Westwood Avenue.

    b. We sent his bill to 654 Westwood Ave.

Answer: b.

Why: Abbreviate "avenue," "boulevard," "street," and so on when writing with complete addresses.

Which is correct?

    a. The post office forwarded his mail to Lincoln Street.

    b. The post office forwarded his mail to Lincoln St.

Answer: a.

Why: The difference here is nuance: Abbreviate only if you mention the street name with the number.

Dates

Here are a few rules to remember when writing dates. Although it looks informal, abbreviate the name of a month when mentioning a specific date:

> We sent you the information packet on Dec. 16, 1995.

When writing the month and year but no date, spell out the month and cut the comma:

> We introduced the plan in February 1990.

Avoid writing a date with slashes between numbers, as in 2/14/97, particularly in the date line of a letter. Instead, write:

> February 14, 1997

Put a comma after the year if the date appears in this form in the middle of a sentence.

Capitalization

Of all writing-related issues, people get most creative with capitalization. Oddly, capitalization rules are pretty basic, pretty inflexible, and pretty easy—once you know them.

Which is correct?

> a. Please ask your congressperson in the Democratic Party to repeal the bill.
>
> b. Please ask your congressperson in the democratic party to repeal the bill.

Answer: a.

Why: Capitalize the names of political parties, rivers, and streets when you write the complete names.

Which is correct?

    a. We have offices throughout Southern Georgia.

    b. We have offices throughout southern Georgia.

Answer: b.

Why: "Southern" is a direction; it's not part the place's name.

Which is correct?

    a. The Department of Public Safety and our company will sponsor the program.

    b. The Department Of Public Safety and our company will sponsor the program.

Answer: a.

Why: With names of large organizations, don't capitalize connecting words. With smaller organizations, capitalize connecting words if they do.

Most everyone knows to capitalize a title before a person's name, as in:

    President Mannings will address the viability of investing in the Czech Republic.

Which is correct?

    a. Lisa Bradley, president of the National Advertisers Organization, gave the presentation.

    b. Lisa Bradley, President of the National Advertisers Organization, gave the presentation.

Answer: a.

Why: When the title is not used as part of the person's name, don't capitalize it. Think of "doctor." You wouldn't write, "I'm going to see the Doctor," even though you do write, "Dr. Robert."

Exceptions: Now look at these notable exceptions to capitalization rules:

- In most cases, don't capitalize such words as "agency," department," "unit," and "area" when they appear alone:

    Please contact the department if you have any questions about the new forms.

- Don't capitalize plural common nouns that follow two or more proper nouns:

    The mayor wanted to appeal to people in both the Democratic and the Republican parties.

- Watch out for words that are trademarks and legally must be capitalized, such as Kleenex, Xerox, and that old standard, Jell-O.

Numbers

Most business writers get confused about when to spell out numbers and when to use numerals. Doing the right thing is important for professional communications. Here are some key rules to remember when writing numbers:

- Write out numbers under eleven. Some people like to write out the number and place the numeral in parentheses beside it, as if the writing would get smudged and the message lost. My advice: keep it clean:

    Our representative sent you two letters over the last three weeks.

- Although half of all businesspeople deviate from this rule, use numerals for numbers greater than ten:

    We have 23 managers on our team.

Exception: When you're beginning a sentence with a number, always write it out.

When writing about more than one of something, beware of these common confusions:

- *Among/between.* Use "among" when you're writing about three or more parties:

  > One of the key issues at the meeting is the competition among our managers.

  and "between" when you're discussing two parties only:

  > Ultimately, he had to choose between two top-ranking companies.

- *Amount/number.* "Number" is appropriate when you're discussing things you can count:

  > The number of people who will attend the company picnic depends on the weather.

  "Amount" is right when you're discussing volume:

  > Since yesterday, the amount of energy has doubled.

- *Fewer/less.* "Fewer," like "number," is appropriate for things you can count:

  > We have far fewer candidates than we expected.

  and "less" is right for volume and degree:

  > There was less toner in the printer than we thought.

IMPERFECT PUNCTUATION

Punctuation is the nemesis of both professional writers and professionals who must write. Some of the rules are confusing. Some seem to contradict others. And some simply don't make sense. Check

---

Believe It or Not

Years ago, when I was a well-meaning college freshman struggling to create that elusive Perfect Paper, I got this piece of advice from an equally well-meaning but misinformed boyfriend: when in doubt, always add a comma. Unfortunately, I was in doubt a lot and wound up with a virtual school of commas swimming through my sentences.

Soon after that, another college companion passed along these breath-stopping words of wisdom: use commas every time you would naturally pause in the sentence. But suppose you have a cold and are gasping for breath? Or you have an asthma attack? You'll end up with commas every four or five words.

The moral of my story is simple: base all your punctuation on logical rules.

---

through this quick quiz of the most difficult punctuation rules. As always, if you get one wrong, read the rule so you can apply it the next time you're writing.

Apostrophes

Apostrophes can be one of the most perplexing forms of punctuation. The basic idea is this: use apostrophes to show that one thing owns, or possesses, another. For example, in this sentence the company owns the logo:

> We decided to change our company's logo.

If you're writing about a payment, you would say:

> Ms. Brown's payment is two weeks overdue.

The apostrophe shows that the payment belongs to Ms. Brown.

Which is correct?

> a. Yesterday, I contacted Mr. Jones' workplace, but he was not available.

    b. Yesterday, I contacted Mr. Jones's workplace, but he was not available.

Answer: Actually, a and b.

Why: When a formal name ends in "s" you can choose either option. The most popular choice, in North America, anyway, is a. If you use b, some people may think you made a mistake. Never change a person's name to accommodate a possessive, as in the incorrect "Jone's."

Which is correct?

    a. We sold Peter and Terry's cars at the fall sale.

    b. We sold Peter's and Terry's cars at the fall sale.

Answer: It depends. If Peter *and* Terry owned the cars, then you write, "Peter and Terry's cars," with one apostrophe for both of them. But, say Peter and Terry owned several cars each, because they were dealers or collectors, then they each get their own apostrophe, "Peter's and Terry's."

Naturally, you don't want to labor your writing with too many apostrophes. So, rather than write:

> We looked up Kathy Brittle's, Caron Savage's, Marilyn Patterson's, and Beverly Dickson's files, then sent them to your office.

write:

> We looked up the files of Kathy Brittle, Caron Savage, Marilyn Patterson, and Beverly Dickson, then sent them to your office.

Which is correct?

    a. We tabulated the voters' opinions and will announce the results at the meeting.

    b. We tabulated the voters opinions and will announce the
       results at the meeting.

    c. We tabulated the voter's opinions and will announce the
       results at the meeting.

Answer: a.

Why: When you have a plural noun that ends in "s," such as "competitors," "affiliates," "meetings," and most other nouns, add an apostrophe at the end to show possession.

Which is correct?

    a. We would be glad to add your childrens' names to your
      policy.

    b. We would be glad to add your children's names to your
      policy.

Answer: b.

Why: Here you have a typical example of a plural noun that doesn't end in "s" and so takes an apostrophe and "s" at the end. Other nouns of this sort are "women" and "men."

Which is correct?

    a. Remember your thank-you's when speaking with customers
      on the phone.

    b. Remember your thank-yous when speaking with customers
      on the phone.

Answer: Surprisingly, a.

Why: This one sneaks into punctuation rule books and is uncommon enough to cause confusion. When you write a word independent of its meaning, you can make it plural by adding either apostrophe and an "s" or just an "s." Here are two more examples:

People want to know how our service will affect them, so put more you's in the opening.

In his comments about the new brochure, he mentioned something about the greens and the blues.

Which is correct?

    a. Three of our managers are former POW's.

    b. Three of our managers are former POWs.

Answer: a.

Why: Whenever you have an abbreviation, with or without periods, you can make it plural by adding an apostrophe and "s."

Beware of Contraction Confusions

"It's" *means* "it is."	Do not mistake with the possessive "its."
"They're" *means* "they are."	Watch for "their" and "there."
"We're" *means* "we are."	Careful of "were."
"Who's" *means* "who is."	The possessive is "whose."

Colons and Semicolons

Most business documents contain colons that serve one or two functions. They may introduce lists:

So we can renew your membership, please send the following:

They also open letters:

Dear Ms. Berry:

Now, look at this third common colon setup. Which is correct?

a. Some of the issues in this month's newsletter are: membership news, upcoming events, and members' suggestions.

b. Some of the issues in this month's newsletter are membership news, events updates, and members' suggestions.

Answer: b.

Why: Only use a colon when the statement completely and naturally stops. If you're really aching to throw a colon into this example, write:

This month's newsletter includes the following: membership news, events updates, and members' suggestions.

Which is correct?

a. Our mission statement focuses on one thing: customer satisfaction.

b. Our mission statement focuses on one thing—customer satisfaction.

Answer: Both.

Traffic Signals

To know when to stop and when to go with punctuation, use this comparison:

Traffic Sign	Punctuation Mark	Meaning
Red light	period	stop
Blinking red light	colon	stop, then proceed
Blinking yellow light	semicolon	proceed cautiously
Yellow light	comma	slow down

Why: They create a more interesting alternative to the flatter, more typical statement:

> Our mission statement focuses exclusively on customer satisfaction.

Semi-colons are also used in two ways. They separate items in a series when any item contains a comma:

> The caterer will provide cheese; red, white, and rosé wines; and cake.

You can also use semi-colons to join two short, related sentences instead of a conjunction such as "and" or "because." This sentence suture can add variety to your sentence structure.

Which is correct?

    a. We received your letter. The issues you raised are important.

    b. We received your letter, the issues you raised are important.

    c. We received your letter; the issues you raised are important.

Answer: a or c, but option c might be the most interesting.

Commas

Commas are perhaps the most widely used and abused form of punctuation. Their function is simple: to separate various parts of a sentence so the message is clear. Unfortunately, most businesspeople go one of two ways—they either avoid commas completely or saturate every line.

Which is correct?

    a. We would like to send you the information you requested, but we do not have the necessary records in our files.

    b. We would like to send you the information you requested but we do not have the necessary records in our files.

Answer: a.

Why: Be sure to include a comma when joining two sentences that contain an actor and an action with "and," "or," "nor," "for," "but," "yet," or "so." If you're joining two short sentences, don't bother with the comma:

> We reviewed the proposals and Accounting calculated the fee.

Which is correct?

    a. On Friday, I received your letter.

    b. On Friday I received your letter.

Answer: Both.

Why: You have a choice here. Some rule books say you should add a comma after one introductory word, others say after three, and still others after five. They all agree that you should use a comma if the introductory word or words contain a verb. My advice: always use a comma to ensure that you're consistent.

Which is correct?

    a. We are looking for an employee who is smart, articulate and can work well under pressure.

    b. We are looking for an employee who is smart, articulate, and can work well under pressure.

Answer: Both.

Why: Again, you have a choice. When writing a list, you can add a comma after the last item and before the "and," or omit one. Here's another example:

> In Europe, we have customers in Spain, Italy, Greece and France.

> In Europe, we have customers in Spain, Italy, Greece, and France.

Which is correct?

   a. Their graphics design chain—GraFix—is not as sophisticated
   as ours.

   b. Their graphics design chain, GraFix, is not as sophisticated
   as ours.

Answer: a and b.

Why: You can use either a dash or a comma to set off information
   that is not important to your sentence. The main difference is
   that commas are more formal than dashes.

Two constant comma problems. Check your writing for these two
comma problems:

1. The comma splice, when you connect two sentences with a
   comma. The problem: the comma is simply not strong enough
   to hold them. Look at this example of a comma splice:

   > We must discuss the plan with the president, she'll have
   > plenty of helpful comments.

   Now look at these possible revisions:

   > We must discuss the plan with the president: she'll have
   > plenty of helpful comments.

   > We must discuss the plan with the president. She'll have
   > plenty of helpful comments.

   > We must discuss the plan with the president since she'll
   > have plenty of helpful comments.

2. A comma separating a noun and a verb:

   > Customers who order before this offer expires at the end
   > of the year will receive two extra pieces of cheese.

   When reading this sentence aloud, many people would make
   a slight vocal pause after "year." Therefore, some people

believe they should place a comma there. But that's analogous to writing:

> Customers, will receive two extra pieces of cheese.

Clearly, this is wrong. If seeing the sentence without a comma bothers you, try rewriting it:

> Receive two extra pieces of cheese by ordering before the end of the year.

> If you order before the end of the year, we'll send you two extra pieces of cheese.

Dashes

Dashes, a useful form of punctuation, have an interesting history. The long dash that you see in books never made it onto the type-writer keyboards of old. So, you now have at least three choices when typing a dash in business writing.

When you type your document in a proportionally spaced font, such as the typeface you're reading now, use an em dash—named because it's the width of a capital "M"—with no spaces around it. The em dash appears nowhere on your keyboard, but most word-processing programs allow you to type one with a simple combination of keys.

```
When you type your document on a monospaced
font, such as the typeface used now, either

    1. type a hyphen — with a space on either
       side of it.

or

    2. type two hyphens——with no space on either
       side.
```

Whatever type of dash you use, remember that consistency is key.

Hyphens

Hyphens, perhaps the most creative punctuation marks, join two or more words to create a single word. Before constructing your own hyphenated words or using a hyphen in an industry term check your understanding:

    a. After receiving your letter, we took your ex-wife, Jennifer, off our guest list.

    b. After receiving your letter, we took your ex wife, Jennifer, off our guest list.

Answer: a.

Why: All these prefixes take hyphens: "all," "cross," "ex," "half," "ill," "well." When it is a prefix and not part of the base word, "self" also takes a hyphen:

    He is absurdly selfish.

but

    Our managers must be diligent, but not self-sacrificing.

Also use a hyphen with the suffix "elect":

    The president-elect will introduce this month's speaker.

Which is correct?

    a. The discount does not apply to non-New Englanders.

    b. The discount does not apply to non New Englanders.

Answer: a.

Why: Use hyphens with a prefix and a proper noun.

Which is correct?

    a. The paper was all-important to the committee.

    b. The paper was all important to the committee.

Answer: a.

Why: When creating an unusual adjective from other types of words, use a hyphen.

Italics

In any punctuation book that's 20 or 25 years old, the discussion of italics occupies a small, practically insignificant section. With the popularity of laser printers, however, italic type has replaced under-lining and makes an appearance in most business writing.

Use italics for the following types of words or phrases:

- Emphasized words:

    It's not enough to grow our business; we have to grow it *fast*.

Italics Tips

- Always check how a publication, even a newsletter, spells its name. For example, the so-called *Atlantic* is actually *The Atlantic Monthly*. Some publications don't include "the" in the formal name, while plenty of others do.

- If you're unsure about whether to italicize a foreign expression, look it up in the dictionary. Don't find it there? Definitely use italics.

- Do not overuse italics. You should use italics to emphasize certain words in sentences such as this:

    Wigwet was the code word they used for the new product.

    However, avoid highlighting mundane or insignificant options, as in this erroneous sentence:

    We offer *more complete* follow-through than any other manufacturer.

- When a rule calls for italics and you are already using italic type, revert to your normal type:

    The sound system was so bad, the sentence sounded like *Gar bluck* Wall Street Journal *geer reef*.

- Names of books, newspapers, magazines, plays, movies, television series, court decisions, and ships:

> The *New York Times* reported that *A Midsummer Night's Dream* was performed aboard the *Delta Queen*.

- Unfamiliar foreign words or expressions:

> The *Kaizen* principle has made our Japanese competitors so formidable.

- A word used as itself, separate from its meaning (you can use quotation marks to set a word off in the same way):

> Donald developed the phrase *parachute response* in that successful ad campaign last year.

Parentheses

Like commas, parentheses set less important information apart from the main message. Since readers often skip or pay less attention to material in parentheses, in most cases you should use dashes, commas, or "such as" and "for example." If you do use parentheses, check them when you proofread! Most people make mistakes, especially with punctuation marks. Remember: You should be able to remove the material in parentheses completely and still have a correctly punctuated, grammatical sentence.

Which is correct?

> a. (We sent the samples to Chase Paper Company on Tuesday).
> b. (We sent the samples to Chase Paper Company on Tuesday.)

Answer: b.

Why: Keep the punctuation inside the parentheses when you're enclosing an entire sentence.

Which is correct?

    a. Customers have been calling all day about the summer sale (they're excited!).

    b. Customers have been calling all day about the summer sale (they're excited).

    c. Customers have been calling all day about the summer sale (they're excited)!.

Answer: a. If the words in parentheses need an exclamation point or question mark, place it inside the parentheses. Then, add the correct punctuation to finish the sentence outside.

Which is correct?

    a. For more information, turn to the list in your employee handbook, (page 7), then call the Human Resources Department.

    b. For more information, turn to the list in your employee handbook (page 7), then call the Human Resources Department.

    c. For more information, turn to the list in your employee handbook (page 7) then call the Human Resources Department.

Answer: b. One of the more baffling punctuation issues is whether you need commas with parentheses and, if so, where you should put them. The rule here is basic and easy to remember: include a comma if it naturally belongs in the sentence, keeping it after the parentheses—never before.

Periods

A period is as simple as it looks: it shows the end of a straightforward sentence. People trained on typewriters traditionally add two or three spaces between the period (or question mark or exclamation point) and the next sentence. However, when using a proportionally spaced font, such as the typeface in this paragraph, type only one space after a period.

A set of three or four periods, also known as an ellipsis, can indicate dropped words or the passage of time. Use three periods to connect parts of a single sentence, four (with a space after each) to connect separate sentences. Don't get carried away and add more periods to indicate a longer wait!

> I've waited for my refund . . . and waited . . . and waited.

> The consultant's report recommends the following: "Show monthly sales figures to the entire workforce. . . . Replace company-wide bonuses with individual bonuses . . . set by supervisors."

Quotation marks

You won't use quotation marks as much as other types of punctuation. Still, by using them—or, more precisely, the quotations within them—you give credibility to opinions, help start documents, make PR material more compelling, and spice up sales and marketing materials. That's because quotation marks distinguish the direct words of a speaker or writer from the rest of the message. The language within the marks also provides a nice change from the narrative voice and gives your readers an interesting third-person perspective.

Here are the basic rules for keeping your quotation marks in the right place:

- Use quotation marks when directly repeating what you or other people said or wrote.
- Use quotation marks (or italics) with unusual or made-up words, and with common words used in an unusual way:

> He thought we should call our children's program "Start-Up."

- Use quotation marks around the names of short works such as newsletter articles. Reserve italics or underlining for longer works:

  > If you want more information about our organization, read the article "What's New at Cabot, Inc.?" in this month's issue of the company newsletter *A Forward Look.*

- Always place periods and commas inside the quotation marks, whether you've quoted one word or ten:

  > According to the radio, progress on the new development was "slow."

- Place dashes, question marks, exclamation points, and semicolons outside the quotation marks when they apply to the whole sentence and not simply to the quoted portion:

  > Why must we "prepare for changes"?

- When you have a quotation within a quotation, set it off with single quotation marks (apostrophes):

  > "The customer asked me, 'Why didn't this machine work right out of the box?' and I replied, 'Because it wasn't plugged in yet.' "

- Normally, you use a new paragraph for each quoted speaker. The exception is when phrases are short and fit together in a single sentence, as in the last example or the following:

  > Students say our adult ed classes are "fun," "a stimulating experience," and "as worthwhile as a trip abroad."

- To insert a clarifying phrase in a quotation, use square brackets to signal readers that it isn't part of the original sentence:

  > Your manual states, "Never flip this switch [the power switch] without first turning off the monitor."

- Some word-processing programs offer a smart quotes feature that makes quotation marks curl like little parentheses (as in this book) rather than uniformly straight up and down (as on a typewriter). This can make your document look more professional. But these programs can mess up. If you don't check to make sure all your quotation marks are facing in the right direction, this feature can make your document look *less* professional.

• Finally, if you have quotations longer than two or three sentences, you'll probably want to set them off as extracts. In this case, don't use quotation marks. Instead, make the quotations separate paragraphs with narrower margins and use smaller or more tightly spaced type:

> But the best reviews for our service come from our customers:

>> You guys are fantastic! I've tried many motivational seminars, but yours was the first that really got me excited! I want to send all the people in my department to your next workshop, and I'm recommending that the company invite you guys to speak to our whole workforce!

TYPICAL SPELLING CONFUSIONS

Another problem for businesspeople is distinguishing words that sound alike but have different spellings and may have similar meanings. Even your spell-check program can't help you here. And there are many examples. For instance, your spell checker can't distinguish between "except" and "accept"—both words sound the same yet they have different meanings:

> He is willing to accept the new position.

> We decided to send the entire department except John.

"Affect" means to influence something, and "effect" means to create a change, or, as a noun, it means the change itself:

> We added equipment to effect higher productivity.

> One beneficial effect of the new policy was fewer lawsuits.

> To affect the organization's future, speak out at the town meetings.

"Already" means before or at an earlier time but "all ready" means completely prepared:

Have you already mailed those letters?

The new materials will be all ready at 5:00 today.

Watch for the subtle difference between "imply," meaning suggest, and "infer," meaning deduce:

The CEO implied that we should expect layoffs.

From all the evidence, we can infer that Hazel has been promoted.

"Principal" means the most important, and "principle" means a guideline or ethic:

The principal characteristic most of our clients share is enthusiasm.

The principal of the business has an office in New York.

The basic principle behind our strategy is relationship building.

"Stationary" means unmoving, but "stationery" is the paper containing your letterhead:

Please leave all company stationery in the storage room.

For the engine to work, the green lever must be stationary.

"Forgoing" something means giving it up, while "foregoing" means preceding:

We will forgo short-term revenue.

The foregoing paragraph shows . . .

Back to Basics

You probably learned these basic spelling rules in high school, but may have forgotten them since:

- Lead/led:

    Even in this technical age, a good manager can lead her team with no more than a pad and a lead pencil. That's the way our founder led his employees.

- Lose/loose:

    With an inventory system this loose, we will lose several thousand dollars.

- Than/then:

    More people use the phone now than they did then.

- To/two/too:

    There were two too many to be seated, too.

Strange Singulars

Sometimes the plural or singular form of a noun is so rarely used that people forget what it is. Here are some singulars (and plurals) to keep straight:

Singular	Plural
addendum	addenda
agenda	agendas
alumnus/alumna	alumni/alumnae
analysis	analyses
attorney general	attorneys general
caucus	caucuses
consortium	consortia
corps	corps
criterion	criteria
datum	data
echo	echoes
focus	foci
genus	genera
hero	heroes
medium (communication)	media
oasis	oases
passerby	passersby
person	people

phenomenon	phenomena
potato	potatoes
proviso	provisos
sheep	sheep
stimulus	stimuli
thesis	theses
VP	VPs

TROUBLESHOOTING

Where Do I Turn?

You know that "Ms." is contemporary. And you know your audience will appreciate "Ms." But your boss insists that you address every woman as "Miss" unless you know for certain that she's married. Or, perhaps you're writing a sales brochure for your company's classes in basketball, swimming, and other recreational activities. Since you're writing for teenagers and the idea you're promoting is lighthearted fun, you want to use contractions. But, your boss crosses out every "you'll" and replaces it with "you will." What do you do?

In the end, you have two choices. One is to determine the company's style by looking at other documents. If no letter, brochure, proposal, or PR piece uses contractions—you're stuck. On the other hand, if these materials use contractions, make an objective and friendly case to your boss. Supposing, though, that your boss owns the company. Depending on your boss's nature, you can either dispense advice or yield.

The Endless Proof

You proof and proof, searching for typos, punctuation mistakes, forgotten words. Yet when the copy's ready for E-mail or the mailbox, you notice that glaring mistake. Yet, what more could you do? Ask someone, anyone, from the mailroom clerk to the third-floor secretary, to read through your document quickly. No spotting for passives. No comments about tone. Simply check for details. Then make your changes.

CONCLUSION

If your document shows careless punctuation, mistaken spelling, and sloppy formatting, what does that say for the quality of your other work? Learn the logic behind the basic rules of English and keep careful watch for problems you've had in the past. When the rules let you go two ways, be consistent within each document. Then print out!

Models

Perhaps the most efficient way to write is not to write at all, but to use models: previously drafted documents that you can personalize for a friendly, professional communication literally in seconds. Perhaps you already have models on file either in your computer or in a pile in your desk drawer. Perhaps not. Either way, follow these suggestions so your models are always fresh, relevant, and personal.

New Models

Most businesspeople falter when they type the first word of their model. For starters, they typically aren't professionals, and they load the document with confusing jargon, incorrect grammar, and other problems that untold others reuse every time the message goes out. So, here's the first rule of model etiquette:

- Consult a professional writer or check other, well-written models before developing your own. Also, check your writing for the numerous issues discussed in this book so your bad habits don't seep into the model base.

The second mistake follows within days or even hours. The well-meaning businessperson creates another and yet another model, crowding the computer with as many versions of one message as Ben and Jerry have flavors of ice cream. Hence, rule number 2:

- Keep only one or two standard models for each message.

The final problem arrives shortly. Another businessperson gets hold of the message. That person reads it, thinks it's pretty good—except for that word there in the second sentence, and, oh yes, that third sentence . . . until this reader has revised the writing. What was a simple stew is now a goulash with dubious ingredients. The next rule:

- Make sure your models are sacred. Individual messages can change, but the originals must remain unchanged regardless of who is using them.

Old Models

It's amazing how long models stay around. Some originated when offices hummed with electric typewriters and computers were reserved for James Bond movies. Virtually every document needs updating, regardless of the timelessness of its message. So, follow this suggestion:

- Clean out your model closet every six months or so, discarding useless models and updating relevant ones.

A second problem is that generations of writers typically invade the model base, especially if no one is around to defend it. The result is that the models wander from one point to the next in an impressive array of styles. They frequently include the styles of employees who have long since left for other positions or even retirement, leaving the models as a legacy of their employment. The best advice:

- Check older documents for consistency.

Finally, old models contain irrelevant information. I've consulted in companies at the top of the Fortune 500 crowd that have sent proposals with incorrect prices. So:

- Update information every few weeks, or more frequently, depending on your business.

The Long and Short of It—Two Model Options

You can't transform every letter or proposal into a full-fledged model. Yet virtually every communication does have guidelines. So when determining the most practical document, decide between these:

1. *Letter template.* This type of model isn't really a model, but a roughed-out idea of how the letter, report, or other document should appear. For example, when answering a customer's complaint, you need to be specific, since every complaint (you hope!) is different. Yet the function of that first line—to reassure the reader through an open, positive tone—will remain the same regardless of the situation.

2. *Complete model.* Put the heart of your message on the page, whether a list of your organization's services or answers to the most common customer questions. Typically, you'll change the first line to address the reader directly and change a few details in the body.

FIFTEEN QUICK-AND-EASY RECIPES FOR THE BUSINESS WORLD'S MOST COMMON DOCUMENTS

The most common written form, whether faxed, mailed or E-mailed, is undoubtedly the letter. And although it may sound boring or difficult, writing model letters is actually fast and satisfying, since each section has a specific and unchanging function. Generally, model letters include these parts:

Introduction: Hook your readers through a personal or provocative first sentence, then provide a compelling action-oriented statement. That way, your readers will already have consumed the nut of your message, even if he or she puts the letter down or skims the rest.

Body: Elaborate on your main point through facts, examples, and other details. The trick here is to create a compelling and logical structure to keep your readers reading.

Conclusion: Make future plans and mention enclosures unless you've mentioned them earlier.

The next section features common letter models, starting with the most agonizing one of all—responses to complaints.

1. Complaint Responses: When You Agree

First sentence of introduction: Apologize for the situation.

Second and third sentences: Let the reader know that you investigated the situation thoroughly.

Body: Explain why the situation occurred and say how you resolved it, whether speaking with the appropriate employee or changing a policy.

Closing: Apologize again and give the reader a number to call if he or she wishes to talk further.

> Dear Ms. Green,
>
> We are sorry about your problem with the seating arrangements on your flight to Phoenix. We spoke with your travel agent, Hazel Walters, who confirmed that she did promise you aisle seats toward the front of the cabin.
>
> Apparently, the problem occurred because Hazel was overwhelmed with calls from winter travelers. In her hurry to help all our customers, she mistakenly neglected to enter your request for specific seats into the computer. In addition, the flight you wanted was virtually filled at the time you called and the front row seats were probably taken. We can assure you that we will make every effort to secure the seat you want on your next trip.
>
> Again, I apologize for this situation and hope you had an enjoyable trip otherwise. If you would like to speak with me further, please call: 555-7869.
>
> Sincerely,

Hey—It's Not Personal

You know the old story—the dissatisfied customer calls and blames you for an inaccuracy or delay that wasn't your fault. Or, maybe it was your fault. But really, you didn't deliberately cause this person trouble and you did, indeed, apologize. So, after listening to the customer talk on and on and on, or after reading one or two ridiculously accusatory letters, you're fed up.

And now, at the apex of your anger, you have to write a response to the complaint. Worse, a polite, even friendly, response. This may feel a little bit like writing a check to some guy who just robbed your house. Before you type a word, remember this:

- It's not personal. In the business world, in spite of often complex social interactions, very little is. Approach the letter as if you were mending a tear in a piece of clothing. Your main objective is simply to patch it.

- Wait a few minutes or longer for your anger to pass. This will help take the emotion out of your word use and give objectivity to your tone. Several employees at one of my client companies like to write a quick yet brutal first letter, working out the emotion. Then, they delete it and write a more objective letter. This tactic is time-consuming, but it can work.

- Think legal. Truly irate customers, whether or not their fury is justified, may call a lawyer. Your document could appear in a lawsuit seeking frightening amounts of cash. That's another reason to keep your message unemotional, even accommodating.

- Compensate. If the situation really did cause the reader inconvenience and your organization was undoubtedly at fault, offer some sort of compensation in the letter—an additional, free service or product or a discount. Nothing soothes a broken heart— or temper—quite like a gift.

2. Complaint Responses: When You Disagree

First sentence of introduction: Thank the reader for notifying you of the situation.

Second and third sentences: Let the reader know that you investigated the situation thoroughly and have found the cause of the problem.

Body: Explain why the situation occurred, taking an objective, chronological approach. Wipe your emotions away, making the message as factual as possible.

Closing: Apologize for the confusion or inconvenience without taking responsibility for it. Then, provide a number for customer questions or calls.

> Dear Mr. McMurphy,
>
> Thank you for contacting us with your concerns about the price of our All-Care Washing Machine and Dryer set. After speaking with several of our salesclerks, we have found the source of the confusion.
>
> The ad that you saw in the *Herald Times* did, indeed, state that the washer-dryer set cost $700. However, the sale ended on August 10—ten days before your purchase. Since you signed the MasterCard sales slip without commenting, we had no way of knowing you expected a lower price. Otherwise, our salesclerk would have discussed the matter with you.
>
> I hope you enjoy your washing machine and dryer and do apologize for the confusion. If you have any questions, please call me at 555-4253.
>
> Sincerely,

3. Thank-You Letters

The flip side of the complaint letter is the thank-you letter. This covers everything from meetings to referrals. Most people run into trouble with sincerity here. Saying you enjoyed speaking with someone or thanking people for their time is so general and cliché, no one actually believes it. You'll jump the credibility gap if you're specific, from the first sentence to the "Sincerely" at the end.

First sentence of introduction: Thank the reader for some specific action.

Second and third sentences: Discuss your next step. Or, as you would in a thank-you for a wedding or baby gift, comment on the situation. "Julie looks exactly like her mother—you'll have to see her soon."

Fourth and fifth sentences: If appropriate, elaborate on the outcome of the help the reader gave.

Closing: Let the reader know you'll be in contact about the results or offer a return favor.

> Dear Judy,
>
> Thank you so much for giving me Stephen Goldberg's number. I called his office yesterday and left him a message. If I don't hear from him by the end of the week, I'll certainly call him again. As I mentioned, having a client like Goldberg Enterprises would certainly be wonderful. They're most definitely our target company and we could help them save money and maximize their processes significantly.
>
> I'll call you as soon as I hear from Stephen. Meanwhile, I'll fax along Maxine Welsh's number. She'd be an excellent contact (or even client!) for you.
>
> Sincerely,

4. Sales Letters

Sales letters are one of the easiest and most common documents to transform into models. Whether you're selling a product or service, a new item or an improved version of an old one, the structure and content of the body remain the same. The only thing that changes is the first sentence of the introduction.

First sentence of introduction (1) cold letter: Think up a reader-focused opening line, preferably one that delivers a benefit. Savings, whether of time or money, always hook the reader. "Saving up to 50% on your gas bill takes one simple phone call." Or, "Don't throw away countless hours on tax forms. Instead, let us do the work for you— quickly and affordably." *(2) when you've talked to the reader:* Establish an immediate and personal connection to the reader by referring to your last conversation. For example, write, "I hope your cold has improved since we spoke last week," or, "Thanks for your insights into DataWorks processes." If you promised to send them material, such as brochures, information sheets, or references, mention that here. Remember, be specific. *(3) when you have a referral:* Mention the referral's name immediately. For example: "Anne Dolan suggested I contact you."

Second and third sentences: Write an action line that will encourage the reader to call you, be aware of your service, buy your product, enlist your service, or make any other response you're after. This is critical for two reasons: (1) to get to the heart of your message in case the reader puts the letter down, and (2) to enhance the possibility that the reader will continue reading your message.

Body: Elaborate on your message, providing details such as prices and approaches.

Closing: Mention enclosures if you didn't in the first paragraph, and make final plans.

> Dear Stephen,
>
> Thanks for all your insights into Maximum Management. As I mentioned on the phone, our management consultants can save your organization up to $1 million a year, while managing your employees' morale and maintaining work flow.
>
> Basically, we take a three-pronged approach. First, we analyze every aspect of your organization from your employees' responsibilities to dollar-to-dollar expenses. Then, we develop a comprehensive strategy for helping you maximize output while decreasing costs within two years. Finally, we work with your

management to implement every aspect of the strategy and ensure success.

The enclosed material includes detailed information about our organization, a client list, and articles from the *New York Times* and other newspapers about our services.

Sincerely,

5. Direct Mail Pieces

According to some sources, fewer than 1 percent of direct mail recipients become customers. So why do businesses continue to send out these pieces? Partly, the success of a direct mail piece depends on numbers. Attract 1 percent of two million readers to a $2-million service and you've made an impressive profit. The trick to these documents is flash—professional flash that promises a concrete, measurable result.

First sentence: Immediately show the reader benefits, using jazzy yet professional language.

Second and third sentences: Write an action statement to entice the reader. If you have a discount, free membership, or any other incentive, mention it here.

Body: Elaborate on your product or service, moving from one benefit to the next.

Conclusion: Mention enclosures and make future plans.

Dear Resident,

For years, you've dreamed of it. A new career. A new life. And now, you can get it, thanks to City University's new program for men and women over 40. Enrolling is easy—just call our 800 number and we'll send an application form. Choosing classes is easy, too—one of our academic advisors will advise you on which of our 200 classes is right for your major.

Once enrolled, you'll also find:

- Affordable classes. Whether you're studying photography or world languages, our classes are affordable; in fact, they're half the cost of most colleges' normal day programs.

- Flexible hours. We know most of our students work or raise families. That's why we schedule evening and weekend classes and independent studies.

- Experienced teachers. All our teachers are full-fledged professors with at least five years' experience.

Want to know more? Call our registration office today. Our number is 1-800-555-2436. Or visit our campus—we're located on Broad Street, just a block away from the City Center subway stop.

Sincerely,

6. Opinions

Maybe you're writing an opinion piece to a newspaper defending your organization, responding to an article about changes in your industry, or promoting a policy or amendment that somehow connects with your line of work. Or perhaps you're writing a letter to customers asking their support for an important cause. Whatever your purpose, be diplomatic. Avoid such words as "stupid," "unlikeable," and other insults. Keep your language as strong, yet even-handed and objective as possible. Always defend every point with a concrete example, and provide a logical order.

First sentence of introduction: Immediately connect with the reader's interest and mention the issue you plan to discuss. You can change this line for each group of readers, whether friends, neighbors, or business associates.

Second and third sentences: Make your point. Include an action statement.

Body: Elaborate on your point, using specific facts, examples, and quotes.

Closing: Tell the reader where to call for additional information when applicable. Otherwise, restate your point as strongly as possible.

Dear Melvin,

As a businessman with strong interests in the community, you should beware of Sam Frasier, a Republican running for state representative. In addition to having virtually no administrative experience, Mr. Frasier has repeatedly voted against plans to upgrade and develop key areas within the West Side business district. Here are a few examples:

- In 1991, he was president of STOP, an organization that blocked plans to create a shopping mall along the West Side corridor.
- In 1993, he publicly called Blear Street "unfit" and "a disaster" and denounced city efforts to develop a strip of shops along Belair and Garden streets.
- In 1996, he led a campaign to withdraw funds allocated to developing the Q-Street projects.

Most recently, he has adopted an image of being a caring statesman concerned with the betterment of our entire city. However, his record proves otherwise. If you would like more information, please call me at The Alliance of West Side Businesses at 555-0987.

Sincerely,

7. Congratulatory letters

These letters are hard and easy to write. They're easy because they're short and so specific that you won't have to struggle for words. They're hard because you must make every message fresh yet may be tempted to use clichés.

Introductory sentence: Congratulate the reader for a specific achievement.

Next two or three sentences: For personal achievements such as a wedding or birth, elaborate on the specific event. For professional achievements such as promotions, state why the reader is deserving.

Closing: If you use one, restate your best wishes.

> Dear Laura,
>
> I was so happy to hear about your promotion to Executive Vice President of Communications. Your background as a writer, as well as your legendary people skills, guarantee you'll do an excellent job. I look forward to hearing great things about you and, of course, to seeing you at those "marathon meetings."
>
> Sincerely,

8. Credit and collections: First letter

Yes, the dreaded credit and collection letter. Perhaps your organization writes its own or perhaps you hire an outside agency. These letters must be strong, yet polite. After all, the reader may have forgotten to pay the bill or may be undergoing temporary financial distress. So, while you *do* want your money, you *don't* want to alienate the reader. Make this a one-paragraph quickie, changing only the date and dollar amount with each new letter.

First sentence: Remind the reader of the amount owed and the date of the first bill.

Second and third sentences: For businesses, ask if you should contact someone else in the business and invite the reader to call with questions or problems. For individuals, ask if the reader has a problem paying the bill and invite the reader to call with questions or problems.

Closing: Express your appreciation if the reader has already mailed the check.

Dear John Dillard,

Please know that we have not received a payment for your $400 bill for a half-page advertisement in the Sunday business section. If we should contact another representative from your office about this matter, or if you have any questions, please call me at extension 1245.

If you have already mailed your check, thank you.

Sincerely,

9. Credit and Collections: Second or Third Letter

First sentence: Remind the reader of your previous communications—phone calls, faxes, or letters—and of the outstanding bill.

Second and third sentences: Offer a payment plan and invite the reader to contact you with questions.

Dear John Dillard,

We tried calling you on April 10 and May 15, and wrote you on May 29 to inform you that your $400 bill for a half-page advertisement in the Sunday business section has been delinquent since February 9. Please call me at extension 1234 if you have any questions or would like us to arrange a payment plan. Otherwise, please send a check to our accounting office.

Sincerely,

10. Credit and Collections: Fourth Letter

First sentence: Remind the reader of your attempts to reach him or her.

Second, third, and forth sentences: Threaten the reader, when appropriate. Otherwise, underscore the importance of paying the bill.

Dear John Dillard,

Although we have contacted you by phone and letter numerous times since April 10, your $400 bill remains unpaid. Unless we hear from you by November 8, we must turn your account over to a collection agency. To avoid this, please send us a check immediately or call me at extension 1234.

Sincerely,

Never Play Truth or Dare

Truth or Dare may be great for adolescents' parties, but it's definitely taboo in the business world. If you make a threat, be prepared to carry it out, whether it is contacting a lawyer or collection agency, or indefinitely cutting off the reader's credit.

---

11. Bios

Bios appear in documents from press releases to newsletter articles to brochures to information sheets giving a person's or organization's background. There are two basic types of bios: the one-pager, which covers every important aspect of the person's career or business background, and the one-paragraph quickie, which gives a tight, specific overview. Whichever type you are writing, be specific, doling out names, dates, and other relevant information. Forget the person's personal life. Bios are business documents, not singles ads.

First sentence: State the most significant and revealing information in the first few words. Titles are great here when you're writing about people. You can alter this line for each new audience.

Body: Provide details about the person or organization in order of importance to the reader. You can adjust this list for various readers.

Closing: Not needed.

Cartoonist and illustrator Mary Lou Larson's work has appeared in over 60 newspapers and magazines around the country, including the *New York Times*, *Newsweek*, and *Rolling Stone* magazine. Her comic postcards, Chit-Chat, appear in bookstores and card shops from Seattle to Miami and everywhere in between. She also has a line of sweatshirts, coffee mugs, and other gift items featuring her cartoon characters. A part-time professor at the Institute of Art, Mary Lou has won numerous awards and contests, including the Arts Council Award for Humor and The Texas Prize for Humor.

12. Press Releases

Press releases, whether one or three pages long, intimidate even professional business writers. After all, the audience consists of pros—the first ones to notice sloppy language or grammatical bruises. The reality of press releases is actually pretty cheery. Newspapers need news and your press release provides it. Editors can simply lift information from your page to theirs, saving their writers for other stories. Press releases have a definite form, each paragraph serving a basic function. All you need to do is fill in the information.

First sentence: Give the five W's: who, what, when, where, and how. Make it exciting!

Second sentence: Provide the essentials of your message.

Second paragraph: Quote someone directly involved with the product or service. If you invent quotes, get an okay from the person you're quoting since a newspaper may end up publishing it.

Third paragraph: Give details showcasing what's new and different about your product or service.

Fourth paragraph: When possible, quote a satisfied customer or other reliable recipient.

Fifth paragraph: An abbreviated bio.

Closing paragraph: Details such as additional phone numbers.

Shape your press release this way:

FOR IMMEDIATE RELEASE
For: Novelty, Inc.
1465 Roseway Boulevard
Florence, FL 09852
Contact: Ned Pierce (800) 555-4321

Larson's Line Hits Gift Shops Coast to Coast

Florence, FL—Now cartoon lovers everywhere can view the
humor of cartoonist Mary Lou Larson in bed, at the breakfast
table, on the subway and street thanks to Novelty, Inc.'s
extraordinary line of mugs, postcards, T-shirts, and other items
featuring Larson's savagely funny cartoons.

"Customers asked us for Larson souvenirs literally daily," said
Chet Miller, owner of Boulevard Gifts in Venice Beach. "So we
weren't really surprised when the first shipment of the Larson
line sold out within a week." He added that Larson's candidly
contemporary humor about everything from midlife singles to
middle-class neurotics has special appeal to his customers.

Larson's line should reach over 300 shops from coast to coast by
mid-December, just in time for gift hunters to find unusual ideas
for under the Christmas tree. The selection includes infant-size
sweatshirts featuring Larson's famous gloomy dog to adult T-
shirts sporting the cartoon character Buzz saying, "I'd diet, but
I'm too hungry."

Cartoonist and illustrator Mary Lou Larson's work has appeared
in over 60 newspapers and magazines around the country,
including the *New York Times*, *Newsweek*, and *Rolling Stone*
magazine. A part-time professor at the Institute of Art,
Mary Lou has won numerous awards and contests, including
the Arts Council Award for Humor and The Texas Prize for
Humor.

Larson's line is also available through mail order. For a catalog that includes 10 other humorists and a plethora of novelty items, retailers and consumers can call Novelty, Inc., at 1-800-555-9786.

13. Reports

Reports are easy to create once you establish a direction for your information. Although you can't cut and paste from one report to the next, you can determine how the pieces will fit in each and basically fill in the blanks each time you write. This works especially well for evaluations and most travel and other short reports.

First sentence: Immediately tell the reader the basics—the reason for the report, the dates of the conference or trip, and other key characteristics.

First paragraph: Provide an interesting summary.

Body: For trips and conferences, provide details in chronological order. For evaluations and descriptions of physical problems such as broken machinery or fire damage, provide details ordered from most to least important, chronologically, or by cause and effect.

Conclusion: For short documents, end with a last point when you've made several easy-to-follow points; a conclusion when you can deduce an interesting point from your experience; or future plan when a clear step will follow. For long documents, summarize the most essential points in order of most-to-least importance.

On September 12 and 13, I attended the Professional Music Educators' conference in San Diego. This year's theme, Intelligent Approaches to Music Education, is especially relevant to our program since we're trying to promote students' involvement in more sophisticated styles of music.

On the morning of September 12, I attended a workshop entitled "Bringing Classical to Rock and Roll." Some of the most important points included methods of showing parallels between the two musical forms to interest the young rock and rollers, and using biographical details to make composers appear more contemporary and lifelike. For example, most young students can appreciate Mozart's wild personality and his tragic demise.

That afternoon, we attended a demonstration concert showcasing the newest methods of electronic composing. Many of these ideas, such as innovations on the synthesizer and creating computerized music with simultaneous images, are groundbreaking and will benefit our technology department.

On September 13, I attended an all-day workshop, "Talking about Music." This provided methods for interesting students in music ideas, from the basics of notation to sophisticated methods of creating harmony, that can add substance and style to their work.

I will write five articles that explore some of these topics for the Music Institute's next newsletter and for external publication. I will also be holding my own workshop on Music Technology, based on the information I gleaned here, at the next faculty conference.

14. Proposals

What do all proposals have in common? They're reusable. One good model, with tweaking here and there, should last years. Otherwise, they run the gamut from four paragraphs to 300 pages, from discussing one service or product to a virtual candy store of possibilities.

First paragraph: Show the reader the benefits of your product or service.

Body: Elaborate on those benefits, show additional benefits, or describe your methods. Focus on time and money savings when possible.

Conclusion: For short documents, end with the last point and prices when appropriate. For longer documents, end with a summary and prices.

Writing Well, Inc., Proposal
for
Gilbert Development

Writing Well, Inc., will meet with your employees to help them improve their writing skills in a series of one-hour weekly coaching sessions in your office. During that time, we will help your employees revise the materials they write every day, such as letters, proposals, and evaluations.

The main focus of these sessions will be to help employees isolate and revise their poor writing habits and use their writing strengths to the absolute maximum. Some of the areas we will cover include:

Active voice. Most business writers use the passive voice, separating the actor from the action. This creates awkward sentence structure, confusing language, and wordiness. We will help your employees identify their passive problems and create a direct active voice instead.

Positive, professional tone. Letters, proposals, and other customer-oriented documents must be as friendly and positive as possible—even when delivering bad news. In the coaching sessions, we will help employees create an appropriate tone to both intrigue the reader and reflect the company's image.

Concise word use. The contemporary reader has a shorter attention span than ever before. That's why our coaching sessions help individuals learn to cut unnecessary words, eliminate tired expressions, and replace clichés with lively alternatives. We also give employees tricks for identifying wordiness without actually reading the document and methods for creating quick revisions.

In addition, we will check for smooth structure and appropriate transitions and will help your employees create professional-sounding letter models whenever possible. The investment in this service is $125 an hour. We can work within your budget and pace the information accordingly.

15. Memos

At last, the memo. That wonderful, short note that you can reel off in minutes. You can create memo models, too, especially when you're faxing or E-mailing similar quotes or lists of instructions. Remember, memos must be short, to the point, and information-packed.

First sentence: State your main point.

Next sentences: Develop the point with support, examples, or details.

Concluding sentence: Not needed.

> To: Ann Marie Doherty
> From: Jennifer Andersen
> Date: September 27, 1997
>
> RE: New acquisition forms
>
> The new forms are located in the second floor closet. They're very much like the old ones except that you must add your phone extension and mailbox number in the top left corner.
>
> Pass the word around to your employees at the next meeting. This is important, since facilities won't accept the old forms after October 10.

TROUBLESHOOTING

Paper Models—In or Out

Some organizations keep their models on photocopied pieces of paper with empty spaces for penning in dollars, dates, or other pieces of information. These do, indeed, tell readers what they need to know. Unfortunately, they're the Kmart of writing: cheap. Worse, they're impersonal, usually speckled from too much copying, and ineffective. Try using a computer model instead, where inserts look like a natural part of the letter. If you don't have a computer at work, have a secretary or other person with a computer insert material according to a standard form.

Model Soup

Perhaps you've looked at your department's models. Not one here and another there, but all of them in one sitting. What you found was an unappetizing blend of styles and even facts. So, what do you do? Before you rewrite, get together a small group of the people affected so you can determine the best approach in terms of style, facts, and strategy. Then, rewrite a few models only, reconvene the group, get feedback, and rewrite the rest. Share these models with others in the company, alerting them to which sentences to edit and how to edit them.

The Last Word

Remember that collection of letters and other documents that you set aside at the beginning of the book? Every so often I've told you to use that file to test some technique. Maybe you did, maybe you didn't. But you should definitely pull out those old documents now.

Compare those letters and memos to the documents you wrote after reading the steps. Do you see how much more powerful your writing has become? Do you remember how much time and effort you had to put into writing before? Now that you've gotten used to the *Words at Work* technique, do you see how smoothly your words flow?

To ensure that what you've learned doesn't slip away, keep this book in the office where you do most of your writing. Mark sections about recurring problems. Every few months, or whenever you face a big writing assignment, flip through those pages to remind yourself of what you've learned.

This book can also help you solve everyday business-writing problems. I didn't have space to tell you what sort of salutation to use in a letter to the king of Norway,* but I tried to answer my clients' most common questions.

Finally, remember that writing is a craft, just as sewing is. Some people are spectacularly skilled at the craft of sewing, while others never manage much more than replacing a button. But we all feel more secure knowing that, in a emergency, we can repair a split seam in our pants. Similarly, we all feel happier and more productive when we know how to make words work for us.

---

*Okay, it's "Your Royal Highness."

Index

About Words at Work

Since 1989, Words at Work has helped organizations transform their writing styles and processes. The result: a stronger company image, fewer calls from confused customers, greater response to sales and marketing efforts, less employee time spent on individual documents, and an improved bottom line.

Words at Work's innovative and successful approaches have been featured in Tom Peters's book *Liberation Management*, as well as in the *Wall Street Journal*, the *Chicago Tribune*, the *Anchorage Times*, *Secretary Magazine*, *Success Magazine*, and over 50 other newspapers and magazines throughout the United States. Among Words at Work's products are ASSET, a unique training and development program, and *Say It Fast! Say It Right!*, a collection of over 250 letter and PR templates that organizations can use to create the right message literally in seconds.

Words at Work's services include assessments and strategies for companies as varied as the Blue Cross and Blue Shield organizations and Massachusetts Envelope, Plus. The company's solutions include style guides, editorial review boards, revised letter templates, and team-writing approaches. For Liberty Mutual Group, Summit Strategies, The Polaroid Corporation, and the Nichols Aircraft Division of Parker Hannifin, among others, Words at Work has provided training in everything from business writing, to sales and marketing writing, to interviewing techniques.

To reinforce training and create a consistent company-wide voice, Words at Work offers intensive coaching sessions based on the documents that employees write every day. As editors and writers, Words at Work staff have helped such organizations as John Hancock, Andersen Consulting, VHB, and Pioneer Investments create first-rate brochures, newsletters, manuals, PR materials, reports, information sheets, and more.

For more information about Words at Work's services, please contact:

Words at Work
20 Park Plaza, Suite 525
Boston, MA 02116
(617) 338-7953
fax: (617) 338-8954